Kindergarten

Teacher's Edition

Senior Authors J. David Cooper, John J. Pikulski

Authors Patricia A. Ackerman, Kathryn H. Au, David J. Chard, Gilbert G. Garcia, Claude N. Goldenberg, Marjorie Y. Lipson, Susan E. Page, Shane Templeton, Sheila W. Valencia, MaryEllen Vogt

Consultants Linda H. Butler, Linnea C. Ehri, Carla B. Ford

 **HOUGHTON MIFFLIN** BOSTON • MORRIS PLAINS, NJ

California • Colorado • Georgia • Illinois • New Jersey • Texas

Literature Reviewers

Consultants: **Dr. Adela Artola Allen**, Associate Dean, Graduate College, Associate Vice President for Inter-American Relations, University of Arizona, Tucson, Arizona; **Dr. Manley Begay**, Co-director of the Harvard Project on American Indian Economic Development, Director of the National Executive Education Program for Native Americans, Harvard University, John F. Kennedy School of Government, Cambridge, Massachusetts; **Dr. Nicholas Kannellos**, Director, Arte Publico Press, Director, Recovering the U.S. Hispanic Literacy Heritage Project, University of Houston, Texas; **Mildred Lee**, author and former head of Library Services for Sonoma County, Santa Rosa, California; **Dr. Barbara Moy**, Director of the Office of Communication Arts, Detroit Public Schools, Michigan; **Norma Naranjo**, Clark County School District, Las Vegas, Nevada; **Dr. Arlette Ingram Willis**, Associate Professor, Department of Curriculum and Instruction, Division of Language and Literacy, University of Illinois at Urbana-Champaign, Illinois

Teachers: **Helen Brooks**, Vestavia Hills Elementary School, Birmingham, Alabama; **Patricia Buchanan**, Thurgood Marshall School, Newark, Delaware; **Gail Connor**, Language Arts Resource Teacher, Duval County, Jacksonville, Florida; **Vicki DeMott**, McClean Science/Technology School, Wichita, Kansas; **Margo Egonhoffer**, Dixon Elementary School, Brookline, Wisconsin; **Mary Jew Mori**, Griffin Avenue Elementary, Los Angeles, California

Program Reviewers

Supervisors: **Judy Artz**, Middletown Monroe City School District, Ohio; **James Bennett**, Elkhart Schools, Elkhart, Indiana; **Kay Buckner-Seal**, Wayne County, Michigan; **Charlotte Carr**, Seattle School District, Washington; **Sister Marion Christi**, St. Matthews School, Archdiocese of Philadelphia, Pennsylvania; **Alvina Crouse**, Garden Place Elementary, Denver Public Schools, Colorado; **Peggy DeLapp**, Minneapolis, Minnesota; **Carol Erlandson**, Wayne Township Schools, Marion County, Indianapolis; **Brenda Feeney**, North Kansas City School District, Missouri; **Winnie Huebsch**, Sheboygan Area Schools, Wisconsin; **Brenda Mickey**, Winston-Salem/Forsyth County Schools, North Carolina; **Audrey Miller**, Sharpe Elementary School, Camden, New Jersey; **JoAnne Piccolo**, Rocky Mountain Elementary, Adams 12 District, Colorado; **Sarah Rentz**, East Baton Rouge Parish School District, Louisiana; **Kathy Sullivan**, Omaha Public Schools, Nebraska; **Rosie Washington**, Kuny Elementary, Gary, Indiana; **Theresa Wishart**, Knox County Public Schools, Tennessee

Teachers: **Carol Brockhouse**, Madison Schools, Wayne Westland Schools, Michigan; **Eva Jean Conway**, R.C. Hill School, Valley View School District, Illinois; **Carol Daley**, Jane Addams School, Sioux Falls, South Dakota; **Karen Landers**, Watwood Elementary, Talladega County, Alabama; **Barb LeFerrier**, Mullenix Ridge Elementary, South Kitsap District, Port Orchard, Washington; **Loretta Piggee**, Nobel School, Gary, Indiana; **Cheryl Remash**, Webster Elementary School, Manchester, New Hampshire; **Marilynn Rose**, Michigan; **Kathy Scholtz**, Amesbury Elementary School, Amesbury, Massachusetts; **Dottie Thompson**, Erwin Elementary, Jefferson County, Alabama; **Dana Vassar**, Moore Elementary School, Winston-Salem, North Carolina; **Joy Walls**, Ibraham Elementary School, Winston-Salem, North Carolina; **Elaine Warwlck**, Fairview Elementary, Williamson County, Tennessee

Credits

Cover and Theme Opener
Judith Moffatt

Assignment Photography
Joel Benjamin
pp. xiv, T6, T13, T17, T21, T23, T43, T67, T75, T77, T97, T107, T121, T129, T147

Illustration
Werner Zimmermann, p. T65; Aaron Boyd, p. T119

Acknowledgments

Grateful acknowledgment is made for permission to reprint copyrighted material as follows:

Theme 8
Cows in the Kitchen, by June Crebbin, illustrated by Katherine McEwen. Text copyright © 1998 by June Crebbin. Illustrations copyright ©1998 by Katherine McEwen. Reproduced by permission of Candlewick Press, Cambridge, MA.

Mouse's Birthday, by Jane Yolen, illustrated by Bruce Degen. Text copyright © 1993 by Jane Yolen. Illustrations copyright © 1993 by Bruce Degen. Reprinted by permission of Penguin Putnam Inc.

Down on the Farm

OBJECTIVES

Phonemic Awareness blending phonemes

Phonics sound for letters *X, x;* review sounds for letters *f, h, k, n, s, t*

Decoding *-ot, -ox* and *-ig* word families

High-Frequency Words recognize two new high-frequency words

Reading Strategies monitor/clarify; question; evaluate; phonics/decoding

Comprehension Skills fantasy and realism; noting important details; inferences: drawing conclusions

Vocabulary naming words; rhyming words; exact naming words; comparisons; singular and plural naming words

Writing story; using naming owrds; journals; friendly letter; class newsletter

Listening/Speaking/Viewing activities to support vocabulary expansion and writing

Theme 8

Down on the Farm
Literature Resources

WEEK 1

Teacher Read Aloud
The Story of Half-Chicken
a folktale from Spain and Latin America by Ivar Da Coll
pages T10–T11

Big Book
Cows in the Kitchen
fantasy by June Crebbin
pages T18–T19, T28–T33

Social Studies Link
Ice Cream: From Cows to Kids
nonfiction
pages T40–T41

Decodable Phonics Library
Dot Got a Big Pot
page T35

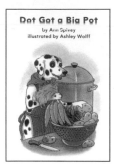

WEEK 2

Teacher Read Aloud
The Enormous Turnip
a classic Russian folktale
pages T62–T65

Big Book
Mouse's Birthday
fantasy by Jane Yolen
pages T72–T73, T82–T87

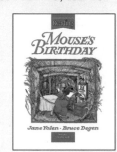

Science Link
Who Lives on the Farm?
nonfiction
pages T94–T95

Decodable Phonics Library
The Big, Big Box
page T89

WEEK 3

Teacher Read Aloud
A Lion on the Path
an African tale
pages T116–T119

Revisit the Big Books:
Cows in the Kitchen
pages T126–T127

Mouse's Birthday
pages T136–T137

Revisit the Links:
Social Studies
Ice Cream: From Cows to Kids
page T144

Science
Who Lives on the Farm?
page T145

Decodable Phonics Library
A Pot for Dan Cat
page T139

Big Books for Use All Year

**From Apples
to Zebras:
A Book of ABC's**

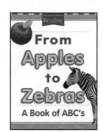

**Higglety Pigglety:
A Book of Rhymes**

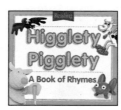

Leveled Books

See Cumulative Listing of Leveled Books.

Phonics Library

Decodable

- Dot Got a
  Big Pot
- The Big,
  Big Box
- A Pot for
  Dan Cat

Lessons, pages
T35, T89, T139

On My Way Practice Reader

Easy / **On Level**

To Fan Fox
by Anne Myers
page T153

Little Big Books

On Level / **Challenge**

Cows in the Kitchen

Mouse's Birthday

 **Audiotape**

Down on the Farm

**Houghton Mifflin
Classroom Bookshelf**
Level K

**Little Readers
for Guided Reading**
Collection K

Bibliography

Books for Browsing

 The Very Busy Spider
by Eric Carle
Putnam 1989 (32p)
Farm animals try to divert an industrious spider from spinning her web.

 Calves
by Kelly Doudna
ABDO 1999 (24p)
Simple text and photos describe the traits and behavior of calves. See others in series.

Farm Animals
by Wendy Barish
Scholastic 1998 (32p)
In an introduction to farm animals, see-through plastic pages change the pictures.

 Cock-A-Doodle Doo
by Steve Lavis
Lodestar 1997 (32p)
Ten noisy animals crow, woof, oink, and moo in this farmyard counting book.

 A Day at Greenhill Farm
by Sue Nicholson
DK 1998 (32p) also paper
When the rooster crows, a busy day begins at Greenhill Farm.

 Big Fat Hen
by Keith Baker
Harcourt 1999 (32p) paper
A hen and her chicks count to ten in this rhyme.

Rosie's Walk
by Pat Hutchins
A hungry fox slinks behind an unsuspecting hen as she walks around the barnyard. Available in Spanish as El paseo de Rosie.

Where's My Egg?
by Tony Mitton
Candlewick 1999 (32p)
Mama Hen searches all over the farm for her lost egg in a rhyming story with split pages.

Big Red Barn
by Margaret Wise Brown
Harper 1989 (32p) also paper
Rhyming text tells the story of the animals that live in a big red barn.
Available in Spanish as El gran granero rojo.

Books for Teacher Read Aloud

* **The Pig Is in the Pantry, The Cat Is on the Shelf**
by Shirley Mozelle
Clarion 2000 (32p)
Eight farm animals make mischief in Mr. McDuffel's house.

Who Wakes Rooster?
by Clare Hodgson Meeker
Simon 1996 (32p)
When the sun doesn't shine to wake rooster, all the animals on the farm stay asleep.

 The Farm
by Gail Saunders-Smith
Pebble 1998 (24p)
A simple photo essay describes the animals and crops raised on a farm.

 My Goose Betsy
by Trudi Braun
Candlewick 1999 (32p)
The narrator describes how her goose Betsy looks and behaves.

Farmer Brown Goes Round and Round
by Teri Sloat
DK Ink 1999 (32p)
A twister roars through Farmer Brown's farm and mixes-up all of the animals' usual sounds.

 On the Farm
by Henry Pluckrose
Watts 1998 (32p) also paper
Photos and text present some of the machines used on farms, including tractors and balers.

Is There Room on the Feather Bed?
by Libba Moore Gray
Orchard 1997 (32p)
A duck, pig, and other animals crowd onto a wee couple's feather bed in this cumulative tale.

 Farmyard Tales from Far and Wide
by Wendy Cooling and Rosslyn Moran
Barefoot 1998 (47p)
Seven traditional farmyard stories from Germany, India, China, and other countries.

 Pigs
by Gail Gibons
Holiday 1999 (32p)
An introduction to pigs, their physical characteristics, and their behavior.

This and That
by Julie Sykes
Holt 1996 (32p)
Cat collects "this and that" from her barnyard friends to make a bed for her new kittens.

Key

 Science

Social Studies

Multicultural

Music

Math

Classic

Art

---

* = Included in Houghton Mifflin Classroom Bookshelf, Level K

Books for Shared Reading

 Barn Cat: A Counting Book
by Carol P. Saul
Little 1998 (32p)
As a cat waits patiently for a saucer of milk, rhyming verse describes the animals around her.

 Let's Go Visiting
by Sue Williams
Harcourt 1998 (32p)
A boy visits his farmyard friends, from one brown foal to six yellow puppies.

 Over on the Farm
by Christopher Gunson
Scholastic 1997 (32p)
Farmyard animals and their offspring star in this bright counting rhyme.

* Cat Goes Fiddle-I-Fee
by Paul Galdone
Clarion 1985 (32p) paper
A cumulative rhyme introduces children to the sounds farm animal make.

 Old MacDonald
by Amy Schwartz
Scholastic 1999 (32p)
Old MacDonald and his entire family appear in this classic children's song.

Z-Z-Zoink!
by Bernard Most
Harcourt 1999 (32p)
A pig whose snoring wakes up the farmyard animals discovers the perfect place to sleep.

Books for Phonics Read Aloud

A Box Can Be Many Things
by Dana Meachen Rau
Children's 1997 (32p) also paper
A girl and her brother pretend a box is a cave, a car, a house, and other things.

Hot Dog
by Molly Coxe
Golden 1998 (32p)
On a hot day on the farm, a small brown dog trying to cool down gets into trouble.

The Fox on the Box
by Barbara Gregorich
School Zone 1996 (32p) paper
A fox eats, plays, and jumps on the top of a box.

No, No Titus!
by Claire Masurel
North-South 1997 (32p) also paper
When a fox tries to raid a chicken coop, a farm dog named Titus finally discovers what his job is.
Available in Spanish as No, Titi, No!

Technology

Computer Software Resources

- **Curious George® Learns Phonics**
- **Lexia Quick Phonics Assessment**
- **Lexia Phonics Intervention CD-ROM: Primary**
- **Published by Sunburst Technology*** *Tenth Planet™ Vowels: Short and Long; Curious George® Pre-K ABCs; First Phonics*
- **Published by The Learning Company** *Dr. Seuss's ABC™; Paint, Write + Play; ¡Vamos a Jugar, Pintar y Escribir!*

Video Cassettes

- **Rosie's Walk** *by Pat Hutchins. Weston Woods*
- **Baby Farm Animals and Friends.** *Baker & Taylor*
- **Let's Go to the Farm.** *Big Kids*
- **The Little Red Hen** *by Paul Galdone. Weston Woods*
- **Farming for Kids.** *Blackboard Entertainment*
- **Hey, That's My Hay!** *Blackboard Entertainment*
- **Sheep Crossing.** *Great White Dog Picture Co.*
- **Petunia** *by Roger Duvoisin. Weston Woods*
- **A Day at the Farm.** *Blackboard Entertainment*

Audio Cassettes

- **The Pigs' Wedding** *by Helme Heine. Weston Woods*
- **Just Me** *by Marie Hall Ets. Live Oak*
- **The Midnight Farm** *by Reeve Lindbergh. Weston Woods*
- **The Easter Egg Farm** *by Mary Jane Auch. Live Oak*
- **Audio Tapes for Down on the Farm.** *Houghton Mifflin Company*

*©Sunburst Technology Corporation, a Houghton Mifflin Company. All Rights Reserved.
Technology addresses are on pages R8.

Education Place
www.eduplace.com *log on to Education Place for more activities relating to* Down on the Farm.
Book Adventure
www.bookadventure.com *This Internet reading incentive program provides thousands of titles for students to read.*

* = Included in Houghton Mifflin Classroom Bookshelf, Level K

Theme 8

Theme at a Glance

Theme Concept: *The farm is a busy place for animals and for people, too.*

Learning to Read

✅ **Indicates Tested Skills**

	Phonemic Awareness and Phonics	High-Frequency Words	Comprehension Skills and Strategies
WEEK 1 **Read Aloud** The Story of Half-Chicken **Big Book** Cows in the Kitchen **Social Studies Link** Ice Cream: From Cows to Kids **Phonics Library** *"Dot Got a Big Pot"*	✅ Phonemic Awareness: Blending Phonemes, *T9, T17, T27, T39, T47* ✅ Initial Consonants *t, k,* and *n, T12–T13, T20–T21* ✅ Blending *-ot* words, *T34, T42–T43* **Phonics Review:** Familiar Consonants; *-ot, -ig, -it* words, *T13, T20, T36, T44, T50, T52*	✅ High-Frequency Words, *T22–T23, T35, T51* **Word Wall,** *T8, T16, T26, T38, T46*	✅ Comprehension: Fantasy/Realism, *T10, T18, T29, T31, T40, T48* **Strategies:** Monitor/Clarify, *T10, T18, T29, T40* **Phonics/Decoding,** *T35*
WEEK 2 **Read Aloud** The Enormous Turnip **Big Book** Mouse's Birthday **Science Link** Who Lives on the Farm? **Phonics Library** *"The Big, Big Box"*	✅ Phonemic Awareness: Blending Phonemes, *T61, T71, T81, T93, T101* ✅ Final Consonant *x, T66–T67, T74–T75* ✅ Blending *-ox* words, *T88, T96–T97* **Phonics Review:** Familiar Consonants; *-ig, -ox, -ot* words, *T67, T74, T90, T98, T104, T106*	✅ High-Frequency Words, *T76–T77, T89, T105* **Word Wall,** *T60, T70, T80, T92, T100*	✅ Comprehension: Noting Important Details, *T62, T72, T83, T84, T86, T94, T102* **Strategies:** Question, *T62, T72, T83, T85, T94* **Phonics/Decoding,** *T89*
WEEK 3 **Read Aloud** A Lion on the Path **Big Books** Cows in the Kitchen Mouse's Birthday **Social Studies and Science Links** Ice Cream: From Cows to Kids Who Lives on the Farm? **Phonics Library** *"A Pot for Dan Cat"*	✅ Phonemic Awareness: Blending Phonemes, *T115, T125, T135, T143, T151* ✅ Initial Consonants *f, h, s, T120–T121, T128–T129* ✅ Blending *-ox* and *-ot* words, *T138, T146–T147* **Phonics Review:** Familiar Consonants; *-ox, -ig, -ot* words, *T121, T128, T140, T148, T154, T156*	✅ High-Frequency Words, *T130–T131, T139, T155* **Word Wall,** *T114, T124, T134, T142, T150*	✅ Comprehension: Inferences: Drawing Conclusions, *T116, T126, T127, T136, T137, T144, T145, T152* **Strategies:** Evaluate, *T116, T126, T127, T136, T137, T145* Monitor/Clarify, *T144* **Phonics/Decoding,** *T139*

Pacing
- This theme is designed to take approximately 3 weeks, depending on your students' needs.

Multi–age Classroom

Related theme—
- **Grade 1:** *Home Sweet Home*

Technology

Education Place: www.eduplace.com Log on to Education Place for more activities relating to *Down on the Farm*.
Lesson Planner CD-ROM: Customize your planning for *Down on the Farm* with the Lesson Planner.

Word Work		Writing & Language			Centers
High-Frequency Word Practice	**Building Words**	**Oral Language**	**Writing**	**Listening/ Speaking/Viewing**	**Content Areas**
Matching Words, *T14* Building Sentences, *T24*	Word Family *-ot*, *T36* Word Families *-ot, -ig, -it*, *T44, T52*	**Using Naming Words** • naming things, *T15* **Vocabulary Expansion** • using rhyming words, *T25*	**Shared Writing** • writing a story, *T37* **Interactive Writing** • using naming words, *T45* **Independent Writing** • Journals, *T53*		Book Center, *T19* Phonics Center, *T13, T21, T43* Writing Center, *T15* Art Center, *T25, T32* Dramatic Play Center, *T33* Science Center, *T11*
Matching Words, *T68* Building Sentences, *T78*	Word Family *-ox*, *T90* Word Families *-ox, -ot, -ig*, *T98, T106*	**Using Exact Naming Words** • naming word list, *T69* **Vocabulary Expansion** • using comparisons, *T79*	**Shared Writing** • writing a friendly letter, *T91* **Interactive Writing** • using naming words, *T99* **Independent Writing** • Journals, *T107*	Viewing, Listening, and Speaking, *T69* Speaking and Writing, *T99*	Book Center, *T86* Phonics Center, *T67, T75, T97* Writing Center, *T79* Dramatic Play Center, *T63* Art Center, *T73, T87*
Matching Words, *T122* Building Sentences, *T132*	Word Families *-ot, -ox*, *T140* Word Families *-ox, -ig, -it, -ot*, *T148* Word Families *-ig, -ot, -ox*, *T156*	**Using Singular and Plural Naming Words** • animal names, *T123* **Vocabulary Expansion** • using naming words, *T133*	**Shared Writing** • writing a class newsletter, *T141* **Interactive Writing** • writing a class newsletter, *T149* **Independent Writing** • Journals, *T157*	Viewing and Writing, *T141* Speaking and Writing, *T149*	Book Center, *T112* Phonics Center, *T121, T129, T147* Writing Center, *T137* Art Center, *T117* Science Center, *T127, T133, T145*

Planning for Assessment

Use these resources to meet your assessment needs. For additional information, see the *Teacher's Assessment Handbook.*

Diagnostic Planning

Emerging Literacy Survey

Lexia CD-ROM

Emerging Literacy Survey

- If you used this survey to obtain base line data on the skills children brought with them to kindergarten, this might be a good time to re-administer all or parts of the survey to chart progress, to identify areas of strength and need, and to test need for early intervention.

Lexia Quick Phonics Assessment CD-ROM

- Can be used to identify students who need more help with phonics.

Ongoing Assessment

Phonemic Awareness:

- **Practice Book,** pp. 225–226, 235–236, 245–246

Phonics:

- **Practice Book,** pp. 227, 230–231, 237, 240–241, 247, 250–251

Comprehension:

- Reading Comprehension **Practice Book,** pp. 223–224, 229, 233–234, 239, 243–244, 249

Writing:

- Writing samples for portfolios

Informal Assessment:

- **Diagnostic Checks,** pp. T23, T33, T51, T77, T87, T97, T105, T131, T155

End-of-Theme Assessment

Integrated Theme Test

Theme Skills Test

Integrated Theme Test:

- Assesses children's progress as readers and writers in a format that reflects instruction. Simple decodable texts test reading skills in context.

Theme Skills Test:

- Assesses children's mastery of specific reading and language arts skills taught in the theme.

Kindergarten Benchmarks

For your planning, listed here are the instructional goals and activities that help develop benchmark behaviors for kindergartners. Use this list to plan instruction and to monitor children's progress. See the Checklist of skills found on TE p. T159.

Theme Lessons and Activities:	Benchmark Behaviors:
Oral Language • songs, rhymes, chants, finger plays • shared reading	• can listen to a story attentively • can participate in the shared reading experience
Phonemic Awareness • blending phonemes • beginning sounds	• can blend sounds into meaningful units
Phonics • final consonant *x* • initial consonant review • word families *-ot, -ox*	• can name single letters and their sounds • can decode some common CVC words
Concepts of Print • all capital letters • left-to-right; return sweep	• can recognize common print conventions
Reading • decodable texts • high-frequency words *said, the*	• can read and write a few words • can select a letter to represent a sound
Comprehension • reality/fantasy • noting details • drawing conclusions	• can think critically about a text • can use effective reading strategies
Writing and Language • drawing and labeling images • shared and independent writing	• can label pictures using phonetic spellings • can write independently

Launching the Theme

Down on the Farm

Theme Poster: Down on the Farm

▶ **Using the Theme Poster**

Sing "Old MacDonald" together, adding verses and animal sounds. In this theme, children will learn about farms and farmers. Ask, *What other animals do you think Old MacDonald might have on his farm? Have you ever been to a farm? What was it like? What animals do you think we'll read about in this theme? What machinery would you find on a farm?*

- **Week 1** After reading *Half-Chicken,* have children explain the purpose of a weather vane to a partner or to a friend from another kindergarten class.
- **Week 2** As a follow-up to *Mouse's Birthday,* have children experiment with size relationships as they can draw animals of different sizes.
- **Week 3** Talk about the foods children eat, and explain how knowing about the food pyramid promotes healthy eating.

Mulit-age Classroom

Grade 1 . . . Home Sweet Home

Grade K . . . Down on the Farm

▶ Theme Poem: "Higglety, Pigglety, Pop!"

Look at the illustration together. Have children describe what they see. Then read the poem aloud. Have children anticipate the rhyming words. Name the animals in the poem *(dog, pig, cat),* and discuss which of these animals might be found on a farm. Recite the poem frequently so that children commit it to memory.

HIGGLETY, PIGGLETY, POP!

Higglety, pigglety, pop!
The dog has eaten the mop.
The pig's in a hurry,
The cat's in a flurry,
Higglety, pigglety, pop!

by Samuel Goodrich

34

Higglety-Pigglety: A Book of Rhymes, **page 34**

On-Going Project

Materials • sentence strips • drawing paper • crayons or markers • fruit and vegetable slices • tempera paint

Foods We Like Potatoes, leafy and root vegetables, and fruits are familiar to most children. List foods children have tasted. Record descriptions and preferences, adding their names to the descriptions. Bring in foods for tasting. Children may change their minds about what they like and don't like as a result.

> Joanne and Lawrence like oranges.

> Keisha and Louis like Spinach.

> Felicia likes potatoes and cheese.

Distribute and have partners work together to illustrate each sentence. Make a class Big Book, "Foods We Like." It's fun to illustrate the book with fruit and vegetable prints. Slice pieces of fresh fruit, potatoes, turnips, brussels sprouts, for example. Dip the slices into tempera paint to make prints. Don't forget to taste the goodies before you prepare them for printing.

Challenge Have children group foods: produce, dairy, grains, and meats. Help these children work on the food pyramid to determine what makes a healthy diet for young children.

Technology

www.eduplace.com
Log onto *Education Place* for more activities relating to *Down on the Farm.*

Lesson Planner CD-ROM
Customize your planning for *Down on the Farm* with the Lesson Planner.

Book Adventure
www.bookadventure.org
This Internet reading-incentive program provides thousands of titles for students to read.

Home Connection

Send home the theme newsletter for *Down on the Farm* to introduce the theme and suggest home activities (**Blackline Masters 111–112**).

Home Community Connection

For other suggestions relating to *Down on the Farm,* see **Home/Community Connections**.

Classroom Routines

Down on the Farm

To introduce a routine...

1. Demonstrate the routine for the class.

2. Cycle every child through the routine at least once with supervision.

3. Establish ground rules for acceptable work products.

4. Check children's work.

5. Praise children's growing independence.

Instructional Routines

Interactive Writing

Interactive writing can be done for a variety of topics: lists, letters, notes, charts, stories, retellings, invitations, a class poem or Big Book. During writing, children are asked to "share the pen." The teacher provides support and does most of the actual writing. Children supply many of the ideas. Interactive writing offers the chance for all children to feel successful as they share their ideas, write words they know, or add punctuation to the writing. Always have children read and reread what they've written.

Independent Reading

In Kindergarten, reading takes many forms and happens in many places. In addition to quiet, self-selected reading time, children can read the poems, songs, charts, chart stories, signs, labels displayed in the classroom. Frequent rereadings of familiar words help children feel like accomplished and successful readers. Label items in the classroom. Point out the words frequently. Have children echo-read.
Then offer children the challenge of "reading all around." With a partner and a pointer, children quietly read the signs and labels, charts and lists posted in the classroom.

Management Routines
Classroom Mail Center

As children begin to write more skillfully and more often, set up a Mail Center in your classroom. Using shoe boxes or large coffee cans glued together, make a sturdy mailbox for each child, labeled with his or her name. Write notes to different children each week. Children will like responding to you. They can also write to a friend. This practical idea underscores the notion that writing conveys thoughts and can be exchanged between friends. Children can also use their mailboxes to hold things to take home at the end of the day. You can use it for notes to parents, newsletters, permission slips, and so on. With the mailbox system, papers get less wrinkled and are not as easily lost as they might be in a cubby. At the end of each day, children learn routinely to check the mailbox to be sure they have their belongings.

Do you have leftovers at the end of an art project? Cut the scraps into small pieces and put them in a box in the Art Center. Tell children they can use the scraps in a new project. If the box is full, put the pieces out on the Art table with a glue stick. Have children make a wonderful 3-D creation from the "found shapes."

Literature for Week 1

Different texts for different purposes

Teacher Read Aloud

Purposes

- oral language
- listening strategy
- comprehension skill

Big Books:

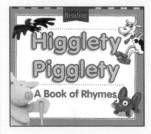

Higglety Pigglety: A Book of Rhymes

Purposes

- oral language development
- phonemic awareness

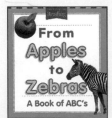

From Apples to Zebras: A Book of ABC's

Purposes

- alphabet recognition
- letters and sounds

Big Book: Main Selection

Purposes

- concepts of print
- reading strategy
- story language
- comprehension skills

Award

★ Oppenheim Toy Portfolio Best Book

Also available in Little Big Book and audiotape

Leveled Books

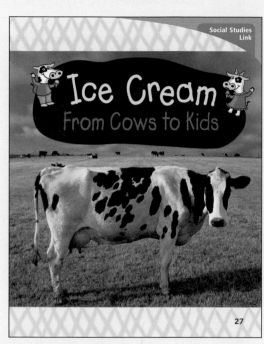

Social Studies Link

Ice Cream
From Cows to Kids

27

Also in the Big Book:
- Social Studies Link

Purposes

- reading strategies
- comprehension skills
- concepts of print

Phonics Library

HOUGHTON MIFFLIN
Reading

Phonics Library

Down on the Farm

Also available in Take-Home version

Purposes

- applying phonics skills and high-frequency words

On My Way Practice Reader

On My Way
Practice Readers

To Fan Fox
*by **Anne Myers***
page T153

LITTLE READERS
FOR GUIDED READING

Little Readers for Guided Reading
Collection K

Katy No-Pocket
MY FRIEND and I
Sheep in a Jeep
Do Pigs Have Stripes?

Houghton Mifflin Classroom Bookshelf
Level K

Technology

www.eduplace.com

Log on to *Education Place* for more activities relating to *Down on the Farm*.

www.bookadventure.org

This free Internet reading incentive program provides thousands of titles for students to read.

Instructional Goals

Learning to Read

- ✓ **Phonemic Awareness:** Blending Phonemes

- **Strategy Focus:** Monitor/Clarify

- ✓ **Comprehension Skill:** Fantasy/Realism

- ✓ **Phonics Skills**

- **Phonemic Awareness:** Beginning Sounds /t/, /k/, and /n/

  Initial Consonant *T, t, K, k* and *N, n;* Short *o* + *t*

- **Compare and Review:** Initial Consonants: *t, k, n*

- ✓ **High-Frequency Word:** *said*

- ✓ **Concepts of Print:** All Capital Letters; Directionality: Return Sweep

Word Work

High-Frequency Word Practice: Word Families: *-ot, -ig, -it*

Writing & Language

Vocabulary Skills: Using Naming Words, Using Rhyming Words

Writing Skills: Writing a Story, Using Naming Words

✓ = tested skills

Leveled Books

Have children read in appropriate levels daily.

Phonics Library
On My Way Practice Readers
Little Big Books
Houghton Mifflin Classroom Bookshelf

Day 1

Opening Routines, *T8–T9*

[Word Wall]

- **Phonemic Awareness:** Blending Phonemes

Teacher Read Aloud
The Story of Half-Chicken, T10–T11
- **Strategy:** Monitor/Clarify
- **Comprehension:** Fantasy/Realism

Phonics
Instruction
- Phonemic Awareness, Beginning Sound /t/, /k/, /n/, *T12–T13; Practice Book, 225–226*

High-Frequency Word Practice
- Words: *a, and, is, here, I, my, see, T14*

Oral Language
- Using Naming Words, *T15*

Managing Small Groups
Teacher-Led Group
- Reread familiar **Phonics Library** selections

Independent Groups
- Finish *Practice Book,* 223–226
- *Phonics Center:* Theme 8, Week 1, Day 1
- Book, Science, Writing, other Centers

Day 2

Opening Routines, *T16–T17*

[Word Wall]

- **Phonemic Awareness:** Blending Phonemes

Sharing the Big Book
Cows in the Kitchen, T18–T19
- **Strategy:** Monitor/Clarify
- **Comprehension:** Fantasy/Realism

Phonics
Instruction, Practice
- Initial Consonant *t, k,* and *n, T20–T21*
- *Practice Book,* 227

High-Frequency Word
- New Word: *said, T22–T23*
- *Practice Book,* 228

High-Frequency Word Practice
- Building Sentences, *T24*

Vocabulary Expansion
- Using Rhyming Words, *T25*

Managing Small Groups
Teacher-Led Group
- Begin *Practice Book,* 227–228 and **Blackline Masters** 176 or 202, 167 or 193, and 170 or 196.

Independent Groups
- Finish *Practice Book,* 227–228 and **Blackline Masters** 176 or 202, 167 or 193, and 170 or 196.
- *Phonics Center:* Theme 8, Week 1, Day 2
- Book, Art, other Centers

Technology

Lesson Planner CD-ROM: Customize your planning for *Down on the Farm* with the Lesson Planner.

Day 3

Opening Routines, *T26–T27*

Word Wall

- **Phonemic Awareness:** Blending Phonemes

Sharing the Big Book
Cows in the Kitchen, T28–T31
- **Strategy:** Monitor/Clarify
- **Comprehension:** Fantasy/Realism, *T31;* *Practice Book, 229*
- **Concepts of Print:** All Capital Letters; Directionality: Return Sweep, *T30–T31*

Phonics

Practice, Application
- Review Consonant *p, T34–T35*

Instruction
- Blending *-ot, T34–T35; Practice Book, 230*
- **Phonics Library:** "Dot Got a Big Pot," *T35*

Building Words
- Word Family: *-ot, Y36*

✎ **Shared Writing**
- Writing a Story, *T37*

Managing Small Groups

Teacher-Led Group
- Read **Phonics Library** "Dot Got a Big Pot"
- Write letters *O, o;* begin **Blackline Masters 171 or 197.**
- Begin *Practice Book, 229–230*

Independent Groups
- Finish **Blackline Masters 171 or 197** and *Practice Book, 229–230.*
- Art, Dramatic Play, other Centers

Day 4

Opening Routines, *T38–T39*

Word Wall

- **Phonemic Awareness:** Blending Phonemes

Sharing the Big Book
Social Studies Link: "Ice Cream: From Cows to Kids!," *T40–T41*
- **Strategy:** Monitor/Clarify
- **Comprehension:** Fantasy/Realism
- **Concepts of Print:** Directionality: Return Sweep

Phonics Practice

- Blending *-ot* Words, *T42–T43; Practice Book, 231*

Building Words
- Word Families: *-ot, -ig, -it, T44*

✎ **Interactive Writing**
- Using Naming Words, *T45*

Managing Small Groups

Teacher-Led Group
- Reread **Phonics Library** selection "Dot Got a Big Pot"
- Begin *Practice Book, 231*

Independent Groups
- Finish *Practice Book, 231*
- *Phonics Center:* Theme 8, Week 1, Day 4
- Writing, other Centers

Day 5

Opening Routines, *T46–T47*

Word Wall

- **Phonemic Awareness:** Blending Phonemes

Revisiting the Literature
Comprehension: Fantasy/Realism, *T48*
Building Fluency
- **Phonics Library:** "Dot Got a Big Pot", *T49*

Phonics

Review
- Familiar Consonants; *-ot, -ig,* and *-it, T50*

High-Frequency Word Review
- Words: *I, see, my, like, a, to, and, go, is, here, for, have, said, T51; Practice Book, 232*

Building Words
- Word Families: *-ot, -ig, -it, T52*

✎ **Independent Writing**
- Journals: Farm Animal or Favorite Room, *T53*

Managing Small Groups

Teacher-Led Group
- Reread familiar **Phonics Library** selections
- Begin *Practice Book, 232,* **Blackline Master 36.**

Independent Groups
- Reread **Phonics Library** selections
- Finish *Practice Book, 232,* **Blackline Master 36.**
- Centers

Setting up the Centers

Management Tip Provide, or ask parents to supply, each child with a shoe box. Label the boxes and store them in the Book Center. Boxes can hold a favorite book, a book that a child wants to read next, and books for reference, such as individually-made picture dictionaries or word banks. Refresh the contents of the box frequently.

Phonics Center

Materials • Phonics Center materials for Theme 8, Week 1

Children work with letters and their sounds this week. They review letter-sounds for *t, k,* and *n.* They make words with *p, d, c, h, n* and the word family *-ot.* Prepare materials for Days 1, 2 and 4 activities. Cut apart the letter grids and bag them in plastic by color. Put out the Workmats and the open the Direction Chart to the appropriate day. Follow the Phonics Center Routine. See pages T13, T21, and T43 for this week's Phonics Center activities.

Book Center

Materials • books about farms and farm animals

In addition to the books listed on page T11, read aloud an all-time favorite. *Rosie's Walk* by Pat Hutchins. A few children may be able to read the book while others will enjoy looking at the pictures. See also the Book Center on page T19.

Writing Center

Materials • crayons • markers • paper or blank books

As a follow-up to their lesson on naming words or nouns, children draw pictures of the parts of a house. Put magazine pictures of various buildings in the Writing Center to prompt discussion. See page T15 for this week's Writing Center activity.

Art Center

Materials • drawing paper • crayons or paints • collage materials • • modeling clay or dough

Children write and illustrate an animal rhyme. Post the chart that lists rhyming words in the Art Center to help children write. They also can make clay models of animals.

Dramatic Play Center

Materials • Blackline Masters 118–119

Children reenact *Cows in the Kitchen*, using masks from **Blackline Masters 118–119**. If possible, make felt masks, using the Blackline images as templates, and have children retell the story using the felt board. See page T33 for this week's Dramatic Play activity.

Learning to Read

Day 1

Day at a Glance

Learning to Read

Read Aloud:

The Story of Half-Chicken

☑ **Reviewing /t/,/k/,/r/** page T12

Word Work

☑ **High-Frequency Word Practice,** page T14

Writing & Language

Oral Language, *page T15*

 Half-Day Kindergarten

☑ Indicates lessons for tested skills. Choose additional activities as time allows.

Opening

Calendar

Sunday	Monday	Tuesday	Wednesday	Thursday	Friday	Saturday
			1	2	3	4
5	6	7	8	9	10	11
12	13	14	15	16	17	18
19	20	21	22	23	24	25
26	27	28	29	30	31	

Locate and name the day and date on the calendar. If you have an outdoor thermometer, check and record the temperature. Have children describe how the day feels. Take the temperature every day for a while to observe weather changes.

Daily Message

Use some descriptive words in your message.

> Today is the first day of a new week.

Play "Pass the Pointer" today. Say a word, give the pointer to a child, and have the child find and read the word. Then ask: **What do you notice about it?** (It starts with *I*; it has only one letter; it rhymes with *fly*.)

Routines

Daily Phonemic Awareness
Blending Phonemes

- Read "Higglety, Pigglety, Pop!" on page 34. Have fun with the title. Say, *Tigglety Wigglety Stop! Bigglety Wigglety Bop!* Encourage more word play and enjoy the giggles from the silly words.

- Then play "Slow Motion." You say a word sound-by-sound and have children blend the sounds into words: /d//ŏ//g/ (dog); /p//ŏ//p/ (pop); /m//ŏ//p/ (mop); /p//ĭ//g/ (pig). Continue with more words as necessary: *top, pat, tag, fit, tip, pot, Tom.*

Higglety Pigglety: A Book of Rhymes, page 34

***Higglety Pigglety: A Book of Rhymes*, page 34**

Getting Ready to Learn

To help plan their day, tell children that they will

- hear *The Story of Half-Chicken.*

- revisit some Alphafriends: Tiggy Tiger, Keely Kangaroo, and Nyle Noodle.

- make weather vanes in Science Center.

Read Aloud

THE STORY OF
HALF-CHICKEN

A Folktale from
Spain and
Latin America

Illustrated by Ivar Da Coll

Purposes • oral language • listening strategy
• comprehension skill

Selection Summary
This folktale, familiar in Spanish-speaking cultures, tells of a half-chicken who leaves home in search of fame. On the way, he discovers how by helping others, one is rewarded in the end.

Key Concept
Helping others

English Language Learners

Review fantasy and realism by helping children categorize books with which they are already familiar. Introduce vocabulary and take a picture walk for children to describe what they see. Also make sure children understand what *half* means. Demonstrate as needed.

Teacher Read Aloud
Oral Language/Comprehension

▶ Building Background

Tell children they'll listen to *The Story of Half-Chicken*. Ask children to close their eyes and tell what a chicken looks like. Ask how many legs and wings a chicken has. Then ask children what they think the title means.

Strategy: Monitor/Clarify

Teacher Modeling Model the Monitor/Clarify Strategy as you read the text and look at the pictures together.

> **Think Aloud**
>
> *I don't always understand what I read. Do you? When that happens, I can stop. I can go back and reread. Or I can look at the pictures. Let's see if that helps us figure out what the title means and what exactly a half-chicken is.*

✓ Comprehension Focus: Fantasy/Realism

Teacher Modeling Explain that some books are about things that happen in real life and some are about make-believe things. Knowing the difference is very important for readers.

> **Think Aloud**
>
> *As I read, I'm going to ask myself if this story could really happen. You think about that too as you listen to the story.*

▶ Listening to the Story

As you read aloud, vary your voice for each character to add fun and drama to the story.

▶ Responding

Retelling the Story Use these prompts to help children summarize the main points of the story.

- ■ *What was special about Half-Chicken?*

- ■ *What good deeds did Half-Chicken do on his way to the city?*

- ■ *How did the wind, the fire, and the water repay Half-Chicken for his favors?*

- ■ *Could the things in this story really happen? How do you know?*

Practice Book pages 223–224 Children will complete the page during small group time.

Practice Book p. 224

Practice Book p. 223

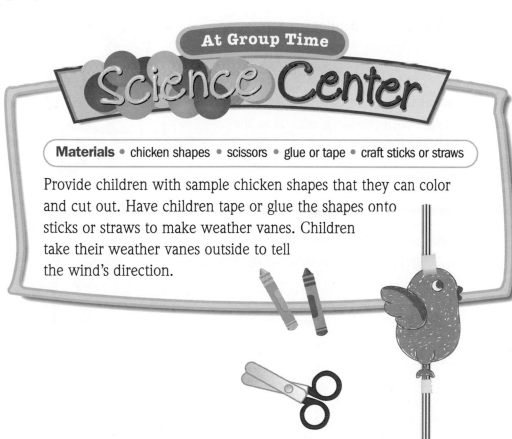

Teacher's Note

Look through picture books about farm communities to find examples of real weather vanes.

At Group Time

Science Center

Materials • chicken shapes • scissors • glue or tape • craft sticks or straws

Provide children with sample chicken shapes that they can color and cut out. Have children tape or glue the shapes onto sticks or straws to make weather vanes. Children take their weather vanes outside to tell the wind's direction.

Home Connection

Take-home versions of the songs for Tiggy Tiger, Keely Kangaroo, and Nyle Noodle are on **Alphafriends Blackline Masters.** Children can share the songs with their families.

English Language Learners
MEETING INDIVIDUAL NEEDS

Demonstrate how a little current of air comes out of your mouth (plosive consonants) when pronouncing / t / and / k /. Have children place their hands in front of their mouths to feel the air. When pronouncing / n /, point out that the air comes out through the nose (nasal consonant).

Phonemic Awareness
✓ Beginning Sounds

⋯⋯⋯⋯⋯⋯⋯⋯⋯⋯⋯⋯⋯⋯⋯⋯⋯⋯⋯⋯⋯⋯⋯

▶ ## Reviewing Alphafriends: Tiggy Tiger, Keely Kangaroo, Nyle Noodle

Use the Alphafriend routine to review Tiggy Tiger, Keely Kangaroo, and Nyle Noodle.

1 **Alphafriend Riddles**

- *This Alphafriend's sound is / t /. Say it with me: / t /. His body is yellow with black stripes. Who is he?* (Tiggy Tiger)

- *This Alphafriend's sound is / k /. Say it with me: / k /. This animal keeps her baby in her pouch and hops around. Who is it?* (Keely Kangaroo)

- *This Alphafriend's sound is / n /. Say it with me: / n /. This Alphafriend is yummy to eat. Who is it?* (Nyle Noodle)

2 **Pocket Chart** Put Tiggy Tiger in a pocket chart. Say his name, emphasizing the / t / sound, and have children echo this. Do the same for / k / in *Keely Kangaroo* and for / n / in *Nyle Noodle*.

3 📼 **Alphafriend Audiotapes** Play each Alphafriend's song. Have children listen for words that begin with their sounds.

4 **Alphafolders** Have children name pictures that begin with the same sounds as the Alphafriends' names.

5 **Summarize**

- *Let's name our Alphafriends and their sounds.*

- *What sound will you remember when you think of Tiggy Tiger? Keely Kangaroo? Nyle Noodle?*

▶ Listening for /t/, /k/, and /n/

Compare and Review: /t/, /k/, /n/ Hold up the Picture Cards, one at a time.

- ■ *Raise your hands if a picture's name begins like Keely Kangaroo's name.*

- ■ *Tap-tap your fingers for /t/.*

- ■ *Nod your heads for words that begin with /n/.*

Choose a child to put the Picture Card below the correct Alphafriend.

Pictures: *toast, key, nose, nut, tooth, kite, nine, ten, king*

Tell children they will sort more pictures in the Phonics Center today.

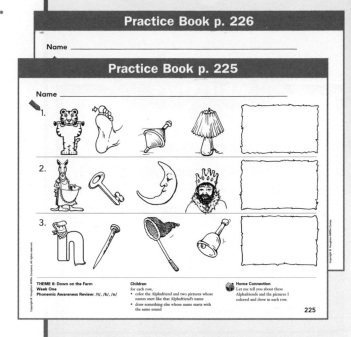

Practice Book p. 226

Practice Book p. 225

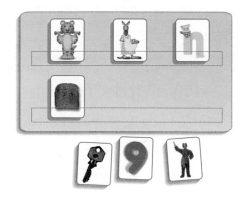

▶ Apply

Practice Book pages 224–225 Children will complete the pages at small group time.

At Group Time
Phonics Center

Use the Phonics Center materials for **Theme 8, Week 1, Day 1**.

Children

- read high-frequency words
- create and write sentences with high-frequency words

- **Word Cards** *a, and, here, I, is, my, see*
- **Picture Cards** *cow, farm, hen, horse*
- **Punctuation Card:** period

High-Frequency Word Practice

▶ Matching Words

- Before the lesson, write the words to "I'm a Little Teapot" on chart paper.

- Distribute Word Cards for *a, and, is, here, I, my, see* to pairs of children. Partners read their word and find it on the Word Wall.

- Say that these are important words because they are often used in speaking and writing. ***I'll read a poem. Listen for your word.***

- Read "I'm a Little Teapot." Partners hold up their card when they hear the word. On a second reading, choose children to find and circle each occurance of *is, here, my, I, a, see,* and.

- Have children recite the poem several times, adding the motions to make it fun.

I'm a Little Teapot

I'm a little teapot, short and stout.

Here is my handle; here is my spout.

When I get all steamed up, see me shout.

Just tip me over and pour me out.

Writing Opportunity Display Picture Cards *farm, hen, horse,* and *cow.* Make word cards for *can, big,* and *pig.* Use these cards to make sentences. Read the sentences aloud, modeling how to punctuate and capitalize. Then have children write their own sentences, using the word cards as models. If they need to, children can use temporary phonics spellings for words of their own choosing.

Oral Language

▶ Using Naming Words

■ Display *The Story of Half-Chicken*. Browse through the pictures, and have children name things they see. Remind children that words that name things are sometimes called naming words or nouns.

■ ***This house doesn't look like the ones we see today. But it has some parts that are the same. Let's see if we can name them. What holds up the outside of a house? What is on the top? What lets us see out of the walls?***

(walls, roof, windows)

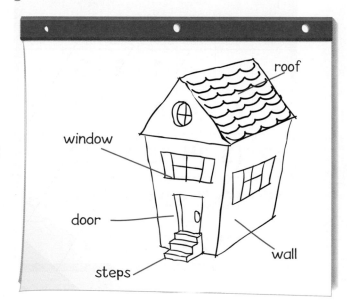

■ On chart paper, draw and label a house. Name more parts. (doors, shutters, chimney, garage, steps)

■ Point to the words on the chart. Read each and have children use it in an oral sentence.

■ Remind children that the words on the chart are naming words.

At Group Time
Writing Center

Put the chart in the Writing Center. Children can use it as a reference for labeling their own drawings of houses. In the large group, have children describe their drawings, using the naming words.

OBJECTIVES

Children
• use naming words

MATERIALS

• **Read Aloud:** *The Story of Half-Chicken*

MEETING INDIVIDUAL NEEDS
English Language Learners

If children are having difficulty naming parts of the house, use questions such as: Is this a *wall* or a *ceiling? Is this a window or a door? Is this a bedroom?* Make stick-on labels and help children place them on a large-group drawing.

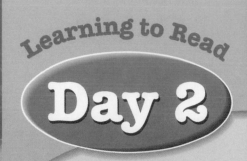

Day 2

Day at a Glance

Learning to Read

Big Book:

Cows in the Kitchen

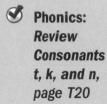 **Phonics:**
Review Consonants t, k, and n,
page T20

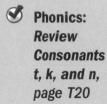 **High-Frequency Word:** *said,*
page T22

Word Work

High-Frequency Word Practice,
page T24

Writing & Language

Vocabulary Expansion, *page T25*

 Half-Day Kindergarten

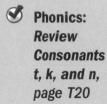 Indicates lessons for tested skills. Choose additional activities as time allows.

Opening

Calendar

Sunday	Monday	Tuesday	Wednesday	Thursday	Friday	Saturday
			1	2	3	4
5	6	7	8	9	10	11
12	13	14	15	16	17	18
19	20	21	22	23	24	25
26	27	28	29	30	31	

By now children can name the day and date. Compare the previous day's temperature with today's. Is it higher or lower? Have children use comparatives to describe the contrast. Model words like *higher, lower, colder, windier, milder.*

Daily Message

Modeled Writing Use some comparative words in today's message.

Today is cooler than yesterday.

Have children chant the spelling of each word on the wall today. *Chant with me:* h-a-v-e *spells* have; f-o-r *spells* for!

✓ Daily Phonemic Awareness
Blending Phonemes

Explain that children will read about farm animals today.

- *Let's get ready for a new book. I'll say some sounds. You put them together to say the name of an animal. Here's the first one: /h//e//n/ (hen). Now listen: /p//ĭ//g/; /k//ow/. (pig, cow)*

- Next, hold up Picture Cards *hen, cow,* and *pig,* one at a time. Say the name, phoneme by phoneme.

- *Now you try it. Choose a partner. I'll say the word. You whisper the animal's name to your partner. Then I'll ask you both to say it.*

Getting Ready to Learn

To help plan their day, tell children that they will

- listen to a Big Book: *Cows in the Kitchen.*

- Review the letters *T, t, K, k, N, n,* and see words that begin with those letters.

- look at books about farms in the Book Center.

Big Book

Purposes • concepts of print • story language • reading strategy • comprehension skill

---

Selection Summary

In rhythmic text, this story tells how animals take over a farmhouse while the farmer naps.

Key Concepts

Animal sounds

English Language Learners

Review farm animals and their sounds before reading the selection. Animal sounds are different in every language. Invite English language learners to share the animal sounds in their first languages. Create a comparative chart of animal sounds.

Sharing the Big Book
Oral Language/Comprehension

▶ **Building Background**

Introduce the Big Book by reading the title and the names of the author and the illustrator. Ask children to name the animals that can be found on a farm. If you have children in your class who live on or have visited farms, let them lead the discussion.

Strategy: Monitor/Clarify

Teacher Modeling Model the Monitor/Clarify Strategy as you read the title and point to the pictures.

Think Aloud

Think about the title, Cows in the Kitchen. *That lets me know that this story is going to be very funny. You've never seen a cow in your kitchen, have you? Let's listen to the funny things that happen. And I'll ask myself if they make sense. Help me do this as I read.*

Comprehension Focus: Fantasy/Realism

Teacher Modeling Model how to decide if the story is a fantasy as you read.

Think Aloud

When I see really funny things in the pictures, I know that the story is not about something that could happen in real life. Let's look through the book to find things that make us laugh. I think they'll be the things that couldn't happen in real life.

▶ Sharing the Story

Read the story aloud, pausing to allow time for children to anticipate and join in with the animal sounds and the repetitive text. Track the print with a pointer or your finger as you read.

▶ Responding

Personal Response Ask children if they like stories that rhyme. Why or why not? Help them understand that rhyme helps them join in the reading.

- *Which part of the story did you like best? What was the funniest part? Why?*

- *Is there a part that you would like to recite aloud? Let's choose one and read it together.*

- *What would you have done if you had been the farmer? Would you take another nap? Why or why not?*

At Group Time

Book Center

Put the Little Big Book *Cows in the Kitchen* and the Audiotape for the book in the Listening Corner for children to enjoy. Remind them to listen for animal sounds. Post a list of animal sounds so that children who are moving toward independence in reading can recognize the sound words.

MEETING INDIVIDUAL NEEDS

Extra Support

Review the Theme Poster, "Old MacDonald Had a Farm" with children. Then make up more verses using the animals and their sounds from *Cows in the Kitchen*.

Extra Support

To help children remember letter sounds, remind them that sometimes the letters' names give clues to the sounds: *t,* /t/; *k,* /k/; *n,* /n/.

Phonics

✔ Initial Consonants t, k, *and* n

▶ Develop Phonemic Awareness

Beginning Sound Play Tiggy Tiger's Audiotape. Children join in as they can. Repeat for Nyle Noodle and Keely Kangaroo. Have children think of a word that begins with /t/ and use it in an oral sentence. Repeat for /k/ and /n/. Children can use words from the songs.

▶ Connect Sounds to Letters

Beginning Letter Display *Tiggy Tiger,* and ask a child to name the letter *t.*

- *The letter* t *stands for the sound* /t/, *as in* tiger. *Say* /t/ *with me. Tiggy Tiger can help you remember that.*

- *What sound do you think of when you see Keely Kangaroo? Nyle Noodle? Who can think of a word that starts with* /k/? *Use it in a sentence for us. Who will do the same thing for* /n/?

Compare and Review In a pocket chart, display Letter and Picture Cards in random order. In turn, children name a picture, say the beginning sound, and put the card below the corresponding letter. If children hesitate, hold up Tiggy Tiger, Keely Kangaroo, or Nyle Noodle.

▶ Handwriting

Writing *T, t; K, k; N, n* Help children review letter forms *T, t, K, k,* and *N, n*. As you form the letters on the board, children use their fingers to trace the letters on their work spaces. You may also want to review the handwriting rhymes for each letter.

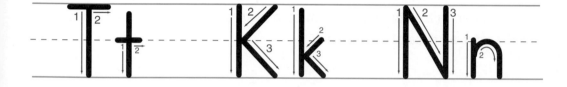

▶ Apply

Practice Book page 227 Children will complete the page at small group time.

Blackline Masters 167, 170, 176 This page provides additional handwriting practice.

At Group Time

Phonics Center

Use the Phonics Center materials for **Theme 8, Week 1, Day 2**.

Practice Book p. 227

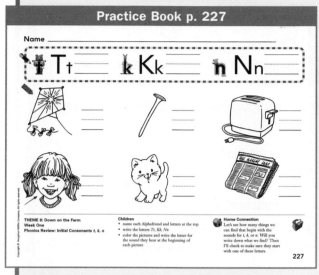

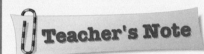

Teacher's Note

Handwriting practice for the continuous stroke style is available on **Blackline Masters 193, 196, 202.**

Portfolio Opportunity

As children show significant gains in small motor control, keep a few handwriting practice pages in their portfolios to document progress.

High-Frequency Word

✔ *New Word:* said

▶ Teach

Tell children that today they'll learn to read and write a word that they often use in speaking and see in stories. Say *said* and use it in context.

The cow *said*, "Moo." The pig *said*, "Oink." The farmer *said*, "Stop!"

Write *said* on the board, and have children spell it as you point to the letters. Lead children in a chant, clapping on each beat, to help them remember the word *said*: **s-a-i-d, said! s-a-i-d, said!**

Word Wall Post *said* on the Word Wall, and remind children to look there when they need to remember how to write the word.

▶ Practice

Reading Build these sentences in a pocket chart. Use index cards to draw a speech balloon for the last word in each sentence. Add a period. Read the sentences aloud, modeling the use of the punctuation. Children take turns reading and add the animals' sounds. Post the chart prominently for children to practice building and reading sentences.

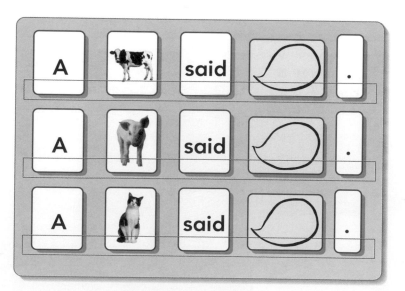

Display *Higglety Pigglety: A Book of Rhymes*, page 14.

■ Read "Little Arabella Stiller" aloud.

■ Reread the fifth line of the poem, tracking the print. Ask children to find the word *said* with their eyes. Then choose a child to point to it in the poem.

Higglety Pigglety: A Book of Rhymes, page 14

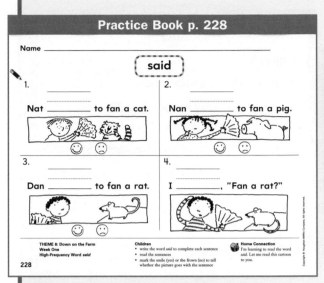

Practice Book p. 228

Apply

Practice Book page 228 Children will read and write *said* as they complete the Practice Book page. They will practice reading *said* in the **Phonics Library** story "Dot Got a Big Pot."

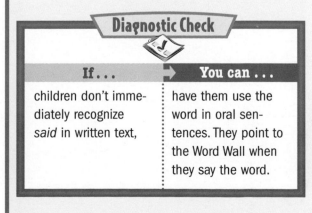

Diagnostic Check

If...	You can...
children don't immediately recognize *said* in written text,	have them use the word in oral sentences. They point to the Word Wall when they say the word.

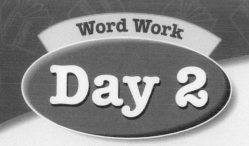

OBJECTIVES

Children
- read high-frequency words
- create and write sentences with high-frequency words

MATERIALS
- **Word Cards** *A, said*
- **Picture Cards** *dog, horse*
- **Punctuation Card:** period

High-Frequency Word Practice

▶ Building Sentences

■ To remind children of the sentences they have been building, reread the chart from the previous activity. Ask who can name more farm animals. For example, *cat, dog, horse, pig, donkey*.

■ Using Word Cards, build *A cat*. Choose a child to read it.

■ *The next word I'll add is* said. *Who can find* said *on the Word Wall? Find it with your eyes.*

■ Add an index-card speech balloon and a period. Choose a child to read and finish the sentence. Have everyone read it together as you point.

■ Build more sentences together until children run out of ideas.

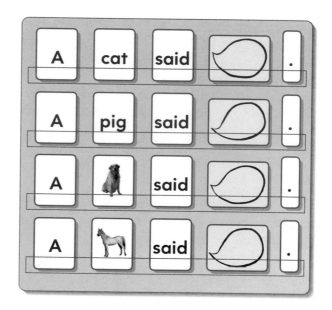

Writing Opportunity Have children think of more sentences they'd like to write on their own, using the chart as a reference. They can use a sentence from the chart or write other ideas. At sharing time, have authors read their sentences.

A cat said ____ .

Vocabulary Expansion

▶ Using Rhyming Words

■ Display *Cows in the Kitchen* and reread the title.

■ *Who remembers what the cow said? What did the farmer say to get the animals out of the house? Say* moo *and* shoo *with me. What do you notice about* moo *and* shoo? (They end with the same sound; they rhyme.)

■ On chart paper, illustrate the animals from the story and help children brainstorm rhyming words for each name. They might enjoy making up a rhyme and illustrating it in the Art Center.

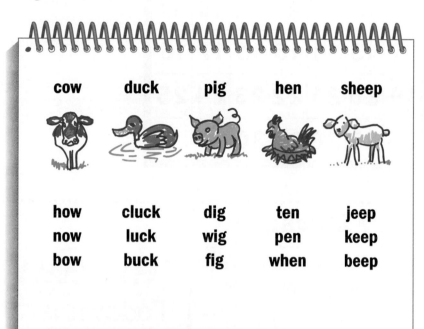

cow	duck	pig	hen	sheep
how	cluck	dig	ten	jeep
now	luck	wig	pen	keep
bow	buck	fig	when	beep

At Group Time
Art Center

Post the chart near the Art Center. Some children will want to illustrate the class rhyme. Others may want to illustrate and label one of their own.

pig   fig

OBJECTIVES

Children
● identify and use rhyming words

MATERIALS

● **Big Book:** *Cows in the Kitchen*

DAY 2

Day 3

Day at a Glance

Learning to Read

Big Book:

Cows in the Kitchen

 Phonics: Blending *p -ot*, page T34

Word Work

Building Words, *page T36*

Writing & Language

Shared Writing, *page T37*

 Half-Day Kindergarten

 Indicates lessons for tested skills. Choose additional activities as time allows.

Opening

Calendar

Sunday	Monday	Tuesday	Wednesday	Thursday	Friday	Saturday
			1	2	3	4
5	6	7	8	9	10	11
12	13	14	15	16	17	18
19	20	21	22	23	24	25
26	27	28	29	30	31	

Choose a child to point to and name the day and date. Then note the temperature and compare it with yesterday's. Is it higher or lower? Have children use comparing words to talk about today's and yesterday's weather.

Daily Message

Modeled Writing Continue to use comparing words to describe the weather.

Today it is warmer than it was yesterday.

Word Wall

Choose a volunteer to point to and read the word that was added to the Word Wall this week. *Are there other words on the wall that start with s? Who can read them?*

Routines

Daily Phonemic Awareness
Blending Phonemes

Play a guessing game.

- Read "Pease Porridge Hot." Have children join in when they can.

- *I'll read the poem again, but this time, I'll stop to ask you a word. Listen carefully because I'll say the sounds slowly. You put the sounds together to make a word from the poem. Remember, don't say the word aloud. Think about it. Then I'll ask you the word.*

- Reread the poem, stopping to segment: /h/ /o/ /t/ and /p/ /o/ /t/. Say each sound slowly, and give children time to blend and guess the word. Check individual responses to monitor understanding.

- As necessary, continue with more words: *not, lot, lip, sap, hat, net, fig, fit, lot, rat, cot, met.*

Pease Porridge Hot

Pease porridge hot,
Pease porridge cold,
Pease porridge in the pot
Nine days old.
Some like it hot,
Some like it cold,
Some like it in the pot
Nine days old.

a Clapping Rhyme

36

Higglety Pigglety: A Book of Rhymes, page 36

Getting Ready to Learn

To help plan their day, tell children that they will

- reread *Cows in the Kitchen.*

- read a story called "Dot Got a Big Pot."

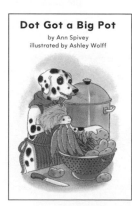

- make clay farm animals in the Art Center.

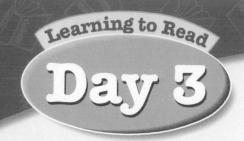

Day 3

Sharing the Big Book

Children

- identify realism and fantasy in text
- understand the use of capital letters in text

Big Book

Reading for Understanding Reread the story, emphasizing the sounds of the animals as they sneak into the house. Pause for Supporting Comprehension points.

English Language Learners

Pause after reading page 7. Ask children what they think a *pantry* might be. As needed, explain that it is a special small room where food is kept. Explain that many houses in the past had pantries, but today most houses don't have them.

Cows in the kitchen, moo, moo, moo,
Cows in the kitchen, moo, moo, moo,

Cows in the kitchen, moo, moo, moo.
That's what we do, Tom Farmer!

pages 2–3

Ducks in the dishes, quack, quack, quack,
Ducks in the dishes, quack, quack, quack,

Ducks in the dishes, quack, quack, quack.
That's what we do, Tom Farmer!

pages 4–5

Pigs in the pantry, oink, oink, oink,
Pigs in the pantry, oink, oink, oink,

Pigs in the pantry, oink, oink, oink.
That's what we do, Tom Farmer!

pages 6–7

Hens on the hat stand, cluck, cluck, cluck,
Hens on the hat stand, cluck, cluck, cluck,

Hens on the hat stand, cluck, cluck, cluck.
That's what we do, Tom Farmer!

pages 8–9

Sheep on the sofa, baa, baa, baa,
Sheep on the sofa, baa, baa, baa,

Sheep on the sofa, baa, baa, baa.
That's what we do, Tom Farmer!

pages 10–11

Farmer in the haystack, zzz, zzz, zzz,
Farmer in the haystack, zzz, zzz, zzz,

Farmer in the haystack,
zzz, zzz, zzz . . .

pages 12–13

▶ **Supporting Comprehension**

pages 2–5

Making Inferences

■ *Where does this story take place?*
How do you know? (on a farm)

pages 6–7

Strategy: Monitor/Clarify

■ **Teacher-Student Modeling** Review how pictures can help clarify the meaning. Prompt:

■ *What happens when you come to something you don't understand? If I didn't know what a pantry was, how could the picture help me understand what a pantry is?*

page 2–13

☑ Comprehension Focus: Fantasy/Realism

Teacher-Student Modeling *So far, we've met cows, ducks, pigs, hens, and sheep. These animals really live on farms. But real farm animals don't talk. So I know that part of the story is make-believe. What else is make-believe? How do you know?*

pages 12–13

Noting Details

■ *What is the farmer doing in these pictures? How do you know?* (The zzz shows that he's snoring.)

DAY 3

> **Oral Language**
> On rereading, note sound words, such as *moo, oink, shoo.* Make a bank of sound words to be housed in the Writing Center.

Day 3

▶ **Supporting Comprehension**

pages 14–15

Cause and Effect

■ *Why does the farmer wake up?* (The dog spills his coffee.)

pages 16–17

Drawing Conclusions

■ *Is the farmer happy that the animals came into his house? How do you know? What does he say?* (No; he is trying to shoo them out now that he knows.)

Revisiting the Text

pages 14–15

Concepts of Print

 All Capital Letters

Point out words with all capital letters on these pages. Remind children that writers use this to show excitement or importance. Read the sentence and have children echo-read it. Then have them find other examples in the book. (pages 24-25)

pages 14–15

> Out of the farmhouse, shoo, shoo, shoo,
> Out of the farmhouse, shoo, shoo, shoo,

> Out of the farmhouse, shoo, shoo, shoo,
> Shoo, shoo, shoo, shoo, shoo!

pages 16–17

> Farmer in the armchair, shhh, shhh, shhh,
> Farmer in the armchair, shhh, shhh, shhh,

> Farmer in the armchair, shhh, shhh, shhh,
> Shhh, shhh, shhh, shhh, shhh.

pages 18–19

Lift the latch, shhh, shhh, shhh.

Push the door, shhh, shhh, shhh.

pages 20–21

Creep down the hall,

shhh, shhh, shhh . . .

pages 22–23

THAT'S WHAT WE DO, | TOM FARMER!

pages 24–25

▶ Supporting Comprehension

pages 24–25

✓ **Comprehension Focus: Fantasy/Realism**

Teacher-Student Modeling *Do real animals come into a house? How do you know?* (Animals could really get into a house, although not by opening a latch; they could mess up a room.)

Revisiting the Text

pages 14–25

Concepts of Print

✓ **Directionality: Return Sweep**

As you reread, track the print. Explain that you are pointing to each word as you read it. At the end of a line, ask children to point to the next word you will read. *As I get to the end of a line, where do I look next for the next word? I move down, and back to the front of the next line.*

 Challenge

MEETING INDIVIDUAL NEEDS

Some children will enjoy playing with sound words, such as *moo moo moo*. Frame a few of them and have children tell the animal that makes that sound.

DAY 3

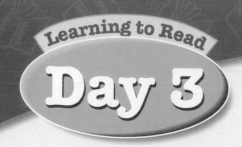

Practice Book p. 229

Portfolio Opportunity

Add selected Response pages to children's portfolios to monitor their comprehension progress.

English Language Learners

Go back through the story. Call on volunteers to name each animal. Then have all the children make the animal sound.

▶ # Responding to the Story

Retelling Use these prompts to help children retell the story:

- *Name the animals in the story.*

- *For most of the story, where was the farmer?*

- *What happened when the animals came into the farmhouse?*

- *If you were the farmer, what would you do to shoo the animals out of the house?*

Practice Book page 229 Children will complete the page at small group time.

Literature Circle Have children select the scene they think is funniest. Ask them to explain what they think is funny about it.

At Group Time
Art Center

Materials • modeling clay • construction paper • markers
• bits of straw or hay (if possible)

- Have children describe various farm animals. Include descriptions of sizes, shapes, colors, and coats or feathers.

- Then make clay farm animals. Make backgrounds from construction paper and markers. Glue on the bits of straw to complete a farm display. Invite another class to come to visit "down on the farm."

At Group Time

Dramatic Play Center

Materials • **Blackline Masters 118–119** character masks

Use **Blackline Masters 118–119** to make animal masks for acting out the story: cows, ducks, pigs, and sheep. Help a child narrate: *Cows in the kitchen..., Ducks in the dishes...,* and the "actors" provide the sounds: *moo, moo, moo; quack, quack, quack;* and so on.

Diagnostic Check

If . . .	You can . . .
children need more practice in discriminating fantasy from realism,	browse through a book about real farm animals. Then compare what these animals do to what the animals in *Cows in the Kitchen* did.

OBJECTIVES

Children

- identify words with initial consonant *p*, /p/

- blend and read words with *c, d, h, n, p,* and *-ot*

MATERIALS

- **Alphafriend Cards** *Ozzie Octopus, Pippa Pig*

- **Letter Cards** *c, d, h, n, o, p, t*

- **Alphafriend Audiotape** Theme 5

Practice Book p. 230

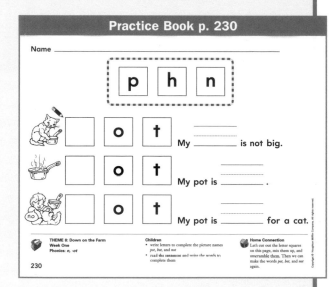

  Extra Support

Show Letter Cards *t, k,* and *n*. Display Picture Cards *toys, key,* and *net*. Children name the picture that starts with /t/ and then find the Letter Card that stands for /t/. Do the same for /k/ and /n/.

Phonics

Blending p *-ot*

▶ Connect Sounds to Letters

Review Consonant *p* Play Pippa Pig's song, and have children listen for each /p/ word. Write *P* and *p* on the board, and list words that start with /p/.

Blending *-ot* Tell children that they'll build a word with *p*, but first they'll learn about a vowel ("helper letter"). Introduce Ozzie Octopus. *Our new Alphafriend is an octopus. Listen, Ozzie Octopus. Say it with me. Ozzie's letter is the vowel o, and the sound o usually stands for is /ŏ/.* Hold up Letter Card *o.* *You say /ŏ/. Now listen for the /ŏ/ sound in these words: /ŏ/ ox, /ŏ/on, /ŏ/October.*

Hold up Letter Cards *o* and *t*. Remind children that they know /t/, the sound for *t*. Model blending the sounds while holding cards apart and then together: */ŏ//t/, ot. The sound for o is first, and the sound for t is last.* Choose a child to move the cards as classmates blend.

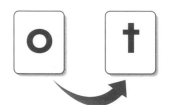
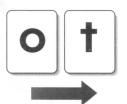

Blending *-ot* Words Put *-ot* in a pocket chart. Place *p* in position. Model how to blend /p//ŏ//t/, *pot*. Have volunteers read as you point.

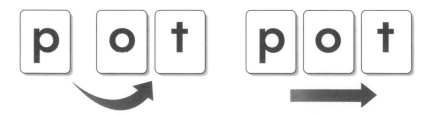

Show how to make *cot* and *hot*. Choose children to make *dot* and *not*.

 Make a word card for *pot* and add it to the Word Wall.

▶ Apply

Practice Book page 230 Children will complete the page at small group time.

Phonics Library

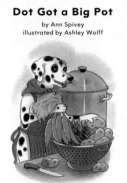

Down on the Farm

Applying Phonics Skills and High-Frequency Words

Phonics/Decoding Strategy

Teacher-Student Modeling Talk about how to use the Phonics/Decoding Strategy to read the story.

> ### Think Aloud
>
> *Let's look at the book first. The first word in the title starts with a capital letter. And I see the -ot word family. Help me blend it. /d//ot/. Yes, it's the dog's name, Dot. Is Dot a good name for this dog? Why? Let's read the rest of the title together.*

During a picture walk, introduce the other characters, Nat and Nan. Point out the ingredients that Dot puts in the pot. Choose a child to point and read page 6. Remind children that they'll read lots of words in the *-ot* family in this story.

▶ Coached Reading

Have children "whisper read" each page before you pause to discuss it together.

page 2 *What is Dot doing?* (She's making soup in a big pot.) *Who will read all the -ot words you see?*

page 4 Ask everyone to point to the word *lot.* Choose a child to read it aloud.

page 6 Ask: *What did Nan say? Who will read it for us?*

page 7 *How does the story end? Do you think the friends like Dot's soup? How do you know?*

Phonics Library

Purposes

- apply phonics skills
- read high-frequency words

Dot Got a Big Pot
by Ann Spivey
illustrated by Ashley Wolff

1

Dot got a big, big, big pot.
Dot got ✂.

2

Dot got 🥕.
Dot got 🥔.

3

Dot got 🌽.
Dot got a lot!

4

Nan, Nat, and Dot sat.
"Is it hot, hot, hot?" said Dot.

5

"It is hot, hot, hot!" said Nan.
"I like it hot, hot, hot!" said Nat.

6

Dot sat.
Nan sat.
Nat sat.

7

Home Connection

Children can color the pictures in the take-home version of "Dot Got a Big Pot." After rereading on Day 4, they can take it home to read to family members.

DAY 3

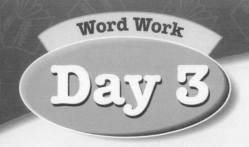

Day 3

Children

- blend initial consonants with -ot to read words

MATERIALS

- **Letter Cards** c, d, h, n, o, p, t

Building Words

▶ Word Family -ot

- Using Letter Cards, have children help you build -ot.

- *Listen: /ŏ/... /t/. How many sounds do you hear? The first sound is /ŏ/. The letter o stands for /ŏ/. The next sound is /t/. What letter should I use? Right, the letter t. Now, tell me how to spell* pot. *Who will spell it for us?*

- *Now let's spell* not. *What letter should I take away? What letter shall I put in its place? Say the word with me:* not. *What do you hear first?*

- Continue making more -ot words with c, h, and d.

Choose children to work in small groups to make -ot words. They can use magnetic letters or other manipulatives in your collection.

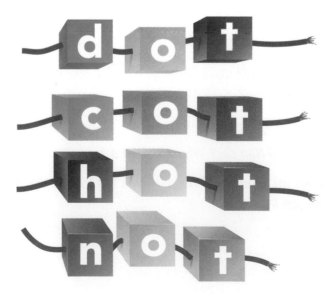

Shared Writing

▶ Writing a Story

Use *Cows in the Kitchen* as a story-starter for Shared Writing. Ask children to think about what they would do if a cow came into the classroom. What would they say? How would the classroom look? Invite suggestions and chart the children's ideas.

Follow the Shared Writing routine to write the story.

- *Kevin would say, "Shoo, cow!" I remember the word* shoo *from our book. It's a fun word and it rhymes with* moo. *That will help me know how to spell it.*

- *Meredith has a great idea. I'll write* pat. *What is the first sound you hear in* pat?

- *What mark should we put at the end of this sentence? How do we read a sentence with an exclamation mark?*

- *How shall we end our story? Who has a good idea? Now we'll all read it together.*

Cows in the Classroom

If a cow came into the classroom, Kevin would shoo the cow out. Meredith would pat the cow. Sarah would tell Mrs. Bond to get a bowl of cow food. We would all like the cow.

OBJECTIVES

Children
- participate in shared writing

MATERIALS

- **Big Book:** *Cows in the Kitchen*

MEETING INDIVIDUAL NEEDS
English Language Learners

Most English language learners will have difficulty with the structures needed to talk about unreal conditions. Provide model stems and help children complete them. Say and write: *If a cow came into our classroom, I would _____.* and *The cow would _____.* Write the children's ideas on chart paper under the appropriate stem.

DAY 3

Day at a Glance

Learning to Read

Big Book:

Ice Cream: From Cows to Kids!

✓ **Phonics:**
Reviewing
Consonants;
Blending *-ot*
Words, *page T42*

Word Work

Building Words, *page T44*

Writing & Language

Interactive Writing, *page T45*

 Half-Day Kindergarten

✓ Indicates lessons for tested
skills. Choose additional
activities as time allows.

Opening

Calendar

Sunday	Monday	Tuesday	Wednesday	Thursday	Friday	Saturday
			1	**2**	**3**	**4**
5	**6**	**7**	**8**	**9**	**10**	**11**
12	**13**	**14**	**15**	**16**	**17**	**18**
19	**20**	**21**	**22**	**23**	**24**	**25**
26	**27**	**28**	**29**	**30**	**31**	

cooler

hotter

As part of your calendar routine, use comparative language to describe today's temperature. Then encourage children to use words like *cooler, hotter, warmer* as they talk about the weather.

Daily Message

Modeled Writing Use comparative language in your daily message. Model how to start the sentence with a capital letter and end it with a period.

> Today is cooler
> than yesterday.
> We'll wear our
> jackets out to play.

Read the Word Wall together. Then play "Rhyme Time." *I'm looking for a word on the wall that rhymes with* near. *Yes, here rhymes with* near. *Now look for a word that rhymes with* red. *Find it with your eyes.* Check children's responses to monitor understanding.

Routines

✓ Daily Phonemic Awareness
Blending Phonemes

Play a guessing game.

- Reread "Pease Porridge Hot" on page 36.

- *Let's put some sounds together to make words from the poem:* / h / / o / / t /, *hot. Now you put the sounds* / p / / o / / t / *together. What do you get?*

- For children who need more practice, continue with more words: *not, lot, sit, pug, fig, wet, ham, man, cot, let.*

Pease Porridge Hot

Pease porridge hot,
Pease porridge cold,
Pease porridge in the pot
Nine days old.
Some like it hot,
Some like it cold,
Some like it in the pot
Nine days old.

a Clapping Rhyme

36

Higglety Pigglety: A Book of Rhymes, page 36

Getting Ready to Learn

To help plan their day, tell children that they will

- read the Social Studies Link: *Ice Cream: From Cows to Kids!*

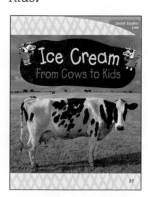

- learn to make and read new words and sentences in the Phonics Center.

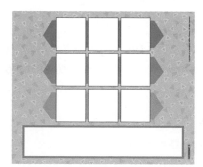

- reread a book called "Dot Got a Big Pot."

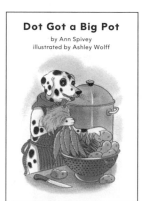

DAY 4

Big Book

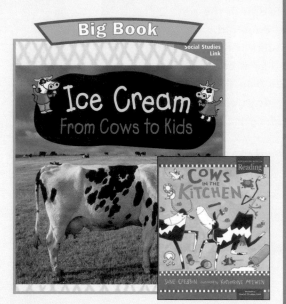

pages 27–33

Oral Language

factory Point to several machine-made objects in the classroom. *Who knows where these things were made? A place where things are made is called a factory. What do you know about factories?*

English Language Learners

Introduce new vocabulary. Guide children in organizing the objects in the order they are used to make ice cream. Talk about other foods that come from animals.

Sharing the Big Book
Social Studies Link

▶ **Building Background**

Read the title. *Who likes ice cream? What does a cow have to do with ice cream? How is ice cream made? What ingredients might be in ice cream?* Have children share what they know about ice cream. Explain that this book shows how ice cream is made.

Reading for Understanding Pause for discussion as you share the selection.

page 28
Strategy: Monitor/Clarify

Student Modeling Remind children that some books tell how something is made. To understand how, the author often gives the steps. Ask: *What could we do if we don't understand the steps?* (Go back and reread; think about what makes sense; look at the pictures more closely.)

 ### Comprehension Focus: Fantasy/Realism

Student Modeling *What do you notice about the cow in this picture?* (It's real. It's a photograph of a cow.) *What does that tell you about this article?* (It will probably be about something that could really happen.)

pages 28–33
Sequence of Events

■ *What does the writer tell us about where the milk goes after the farmer milks the cows?* (to the factory) *What happens before the ice cream is frozen?* (It's put into cups.)

page 30
Noting Details

■ *What is ice cream made from?* (milk and sugar)

A farmer milked the cow in the barn, moo, moo, moo.

A truck carried the milk to the factory, slosh, slosh, slosh.

28

29

pages 28–29

A worker mixed the milk with sugar, swish, swish, swish.

A machine poured the ice cream into a cup, glop, glop, glop.

30

31

pages 30–31

A freezer froze the ice cream in the factory, brr, brr, brr.

A truck carried the ice cream to the children. They said, "Yum, yum, yum!"

32

33

pages 32–33

Revisiting the Text

pages 30–31

Concepts of Print

 Directionality: Return Sweep

■ Reread the first sentence on page 31, pointing as you read to confirm directionality. Choose a child to demonstrate the direction on another page as you read aloud.

▶ Responding

Summarizing To help children summmarize the selection, discuss the ice cream-making process together, and be sure to use words like *First*, *then*, and *at the end*.

MEETING INDIVIDUAL NEEDS Challenge

Children who are ready for a challenge can describe and draw the steps for making another familiar food, for example, chocolate pudding, pancakes, scrambled eggs. Children can number and label the steps.

DAY 4

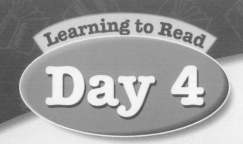

Teacher's Note

As they write, children may ask how to spell words from the *-ot* family. Help them find *pot* on the Word Wall and substitute the appropriate initial consonant.

Home Connection

Ask parents to search for foods that begin with *t* and *n* in the grocery store. They can send in the results of the search.

Phonics

Blending -ot Words

▶ Connect Sounds to Letters

Review Consonants *p, n* Display page 17 of *From Apples to Zebras*. Talk about the pig. Compare it with Alphafriend *Pippa Pig*. Then focus on the initial *p*. Do the same with the noodle on page 15, focusing on the initial sounds and letters.

Reviewing *-ot* Remind children that to build words with *p* or *n*, they also need a vowel ("helper letter"), because every word has at least one of those. Ask which Alphafriend stands for the vowel sound /ŏ/. (Ozzie Octopus) Display Ozzie and have children think of other words that start with /ŏ/. (*October, on, otter,* and *ox*)

pig   popcorn

pear   pizza

17

***From Apples to Zebras: A Book of ABC's*, page 17**

Hold up Letter Cards *p, o,* and *t. Watch and listen as I build a word from the Word Wall:* / p // ŏ // t /, pot.

Blending *-ot* Words Put the Letter Card *n* in front of *-ot. Now let's blend a new word:* / n // ot /, not. Continue, choosing children to build and blend *cot, got,* and *dot.*

▶ Apply

In the pocket chart, make *pot* with Letter Cards. Children change *pot* to *hot* by adding *h.* Now build sentences like the ones shown.

For *got*, ask what letter you need to spell each sound. Choose a child to read the sentence and blend the *-ot* word.

Practice Book page 231 Children will complete this page at small group time.

Phonics Library In groups today, children will also read *-ot* words as they reread the **Phonics Library** story "Dot Got a Big Pot." See suggestions, page T35.

Use the Phonics Center materials for **Theme 8, Week 1, Day 4**.

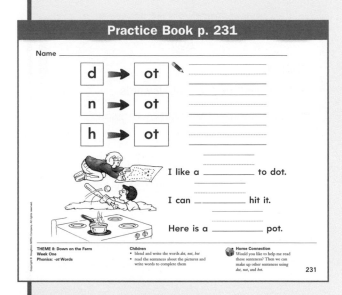

Portfolio Opportunity

In your conferences with children, decide together on a Practice Book page to save in the portfolio and then share with parents.

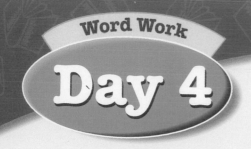

Children

• build and read *-ot, -ig, -it* words

MATERIALS

• **Letter Cards** *b, d, f, g, h, i, l, n, o, p, t*

Building Words

▶ Word Families: *-ot,- ig, -it*

Model how to build *pot* in a pocket chart, saying sounds slowly and writing what you hear. ***Let's build the word* pot*. Which letter should I put first? Next? Last? Remember that saying a word slowly helps us know how it's spelled.***

Praise children's growing reading skills. Point out that now they can make lots of words because of all the letters and sounds they've learned. Demonstrate by helping them write words with *-ot, -ig, -it* and *b, d, f, g, h, l, n, p.*

Children use magnetic letters or other manipulatives in your collection to build *-ot, -ig,* and *-it* words. They can keep a list of their words to read to a partner.

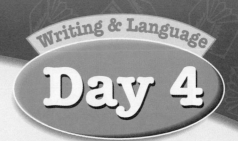

Interactive Writing

▶ Using Naming Words

■ Remind children that naming words, or nouns, tell about a place or person. Ask children to think about and name their favorite rooms in a house. You could start the discussion by describing a room where you like to be.

■ Begin with a sentence stem like the one shown.

■ Writing becomes interactive when children "share the pen" to add a suggested word, consonant, name, or high-frequency word. They can add punctuation, too. Follow the Interactive Writing Routine as you write with children.

■ *What is your favorite room? I like the kitchen best, so I'll write that. I'll write my name. Who will write the first letter in the word* kitchen?

■ *Anja likes the den.* (Anja writes her name.) *Who will tell Anja how to spell* den?

■ *Kevin likes the bedroom. Let's listen to that word. Clap it.* (bed-room) *How many words do you hear? Who can write* bed? *I'll finish it for you.*

Our Favorite Rooms

Mrs. Chavez likes the kitchen.
Anja likes the den best.
Kevin likes the bedroom best.
Willy likes the kitchen, too.
Lisa likes all the rooms.

Kevin and k

DAY 4

English Language Learners

As children talk about their favorite rooms, check for use of the article *the.* As needed, explain that *the* can be used with words that mean one or more than one: *the room, the rooms; a* and *an* are used only with singular naming words: *a window, an office.*

Learning to Read
Day 5

Day at a Glance

Learning to Read

Revisiting the Literature:

The Story of Half-Chicken, Cows in the Kitchen, Ice Cream: From Cows to Kids!, "Dot Got a Big Pot"

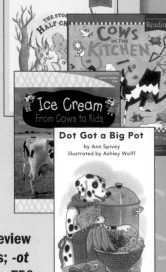

Dot Got a Big Pot
by Ann Spivey
illustrated by Ashley Wolff

☑ **Phonics: Review Consonants; -ot Words;** *page T50*

Word Work

Building Words, *page T52*

Writing & Language

Independent Writing, *page T53*

 Half-Day Kindergarten

☑ Indicates lessons for tested skills. Choose additional activities as time allows.

Opening

Calendar

Sunday	Monday	Tuesday	Wednesday	Thursday	Friday	Saturday
			1	2	3	4
5	6	7	8	9	10	11
12	13	14	15	16	17	18
19	20	21	22	23	24	25
26	27	28	29	30	31	

Read the thermometer to get the day's temperature, and compare it to readings taken on previous days. Which temperature was highest? lowest? Help children relate the temperature to comparative words like *warmest* and *coolest.*

Daily Message

Interactive Writing Share the pen: In the daily message, occasionally ask volunteers to contribute words or letters they can read and write.

Monday was the coldest day.

Read the Word Wall together. Then play a guessing game: *I'm thinking of a word that has four letters and starts with / s /. Who can find and read that word for us?* Continue with similar clues for other words.

Routines

 Daily Phonemic Awareness
Blending Phonemes

- Display the Picture Cards for *pan, pig,* and *pot.* Have children name the pictures, noting that they all begin with the same sound.

- *Listen carefully. I'm going to say some sounds. You put them together to make a word for one of the pictures. Remember: All the words begin with the same sound. Listen really hard for the middle and end sounds. /p/ /an/; /p/ /ig/; /p/ /ot/.*

- For more words, use *fat, fig,* and *fog; ten, tan,* and *top; win, wag,* and *wet.*

Getting Ready to Learn

To help plan their day, tell children that they will

- reread and talk about all the books they've read this week.

- take home a story they can read.

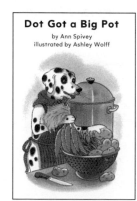

Dot Got a Big Pot
by Ann Spivey
illustrated by Ashley Wolff

- write in their journals.

My Journal

DAY 5

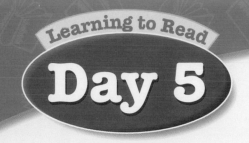

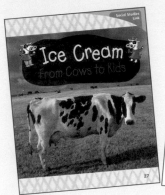

Revisiting the Literature

▶ Literature Discussion

Today children will compare books you've shared this week: *The Story of Half-Chicken, Cows in the Kitchen, Ice Cream: From Cows to Kids!,* and the decodable story "Dot Got a Big Pot." First, use these suggestions to help children recall the books:

- Have volunteers show and tell about the times Half-Chicken helped others in *The Story of Half-Chicken.*

- Children view the illustrations and name one or two settings from *Cows in the Kitchen* (kitchen, pantry, dishes, hat stand). Select children to describe what the animals are doing in each picture.

- Reread page 28 from *Ice Cream: From Cows to Kids!,* and choose a child to tell what happens next.

- Look through "Dot Got a Big Pot." Choose a child to model for the group how to read *got, Dot,* or *pot.* Ask children to read the story to a partner during small group time.

- Ask children to vote for their favorite book of the week. Reread the text of the winner aloud.

Comprehension: Fantasy/Realism

Comparing Books Remind children that they have learned to think about whether the events in a story could really happen. Browse through each selection with children, inviting comments about whether the actions are realistic or make-believe. Encourage children to support their reasoning.

Technology

www.eduplace.com
Log on to **Education Place** for more activities relating to Down on the Farm.

www.bookadventure.org
This internet reading-incentive program provides thousands of titles for children to read.

Building Fluency

▶ Rereading Familiar Texts

Phonics Library: "Dot Got a Big Pot" Remind children that they've learned the new word *said* this week, and that they've learned to read words with *-ot*. As they reread "Dot Got a Big Pot," have children look for words with *-ot*.

Review Feature several familiar **Phonics Library** titles in the Book Center. Have children demonstrate their growing skills by choosing one to reread aloud. Children can alternate pages with a partner.

Oral Reading Frequent rereadings of familiar texts help children develop a smoothness and fewer pauses between words in their oral reading. Model often how to read smoothly in phrases, pausing for end punctuation. Then have children try it.

Dot Got a Big Pot
by Ann Spivey
illustrated by Ashley Wolff

Zig Pig and Dan Cat
by Amy Griffin
illustrated by Amiko Hirao

Tan Van
by Amy Griffin
illustrated by Amiko Hirao

Blackline Master 136 Children complete the page and take it home to share their reading progress.

My Reading Log

I can read

My new words

said pot

Leveled Books

The materials listed below provide reading practice for children at different levels.

Little Big Books

Little Readers for Guided Reading

Houghton Mifflin Classroom Bookshelf

Home Connection

Remind children to share the take-home version of "Dot Got a Big Pot" with their families.

Revisiting the Literature/ Building Fluency

DAY 5

Phonics Review
✓ Consonants, Word Families

▶ Review

Tell children that they'll take turns being word builders and word readers today. Have word builders stand with you at the chalkboard.

■ *Let's build pot. First, count the sounds ... I know p stands for /p/ and o stands for /ŏ/, and t stands for /t/.*

■ Choose a child to write *pot* on the board. Word readers read it.

■ Change *p* to *n*. Children write the word and ask the word readers to read it.

■ Continue until everyone builds a word by replacing one letter. Examples: *hot, cot, dot, got; big, pig, fig; lit, kit, sit.*

High-Frequency Word Review

✓ *I, see, my, like, a, to, and, go, is, here, for, have, said*

▶ Review

Give each small group the Word Cards, Picture Cards, and Punctuation Card needed to make a sentence. Each child holds one card. Children stand and arrange themselves to make a sentence for others to read.

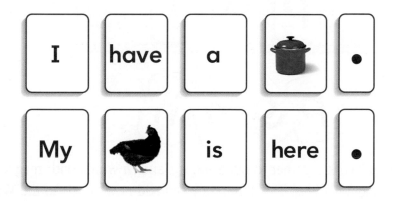

▶ Apply

Practice Book page 232 Children can complete this page independently and read it to you during small group time.

Phonics Library Have children take turns reading aloud to the class. Each child might read one page of "Dot Got a Big Pot" or a favorite **Phonics Library** selection from the previous theme. Remind readers to share the pictures!

Questions for discussion:

■ *Do you hear any rhyming words in either story? What letters are the same in those words?*

■ *Find a word that starts with the same sound as Tiggy Tiger's name. What is the letter? What is the sound?* Do the same for Keely Kangaroo and Nyle Noodle.

■ *This week we added* said *to the Word Wall. Find* said *in "Dot Got a Big Pot."*

Practice Book p. 232

Portfolio Opportunity

Save the Practice Book page to share with parents at conference time.

Diagnostic Check

If . . .	You can . . .
children need help remembering letter sounds,	have them color and name the BLM version of the specific Alphafriend.
children pause at high-frequency words when reading,	have them find these words with a partner on the Word Wall.

DAY 5

OBJECTIVES

Children

- build and read -ot, -ig, and -it words

MATERIALS

- **Letter Cards** c, d, g, h, n, o, p, t

Building Words

▶ Word Families: *-ot, -ig, -it*

Model how to build *-ot.* Along the bottom of a pocket chart, line up the letters *p, g, d, c, n,* and *h.* **Let's build the word** dot. **Who can tell me which letter I should take from here to make** dot? Have a volunteer take the letter *d* and place it in front of *-ot.* Continue building *-ot* words, using initial consonants *n, c, g, p,* and *h.* On chart paper, keep a list of all the *-ot* words you make, and reread the list together.

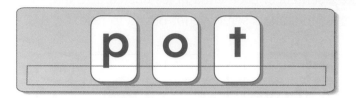

Have small groups work together to build *-ot, -ig,* and *-it* words with magnetic letters or other manipulatives. This time, they can add new words to the Word Bank section of their journals and draw appropriate pictures.

Independent Writing

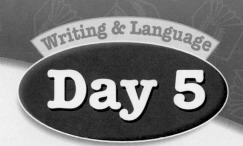
▶ Journals

Volunteers can read this week's shared and interactive writing posted in the classroom. Encourage children to work independently. If they need an idea to get started, you could suggest they write about a farm animal or a favorite room.

- *What is your favorite room at school or in your grandmother's house? Why is it your favorite?*

- *We've been talking about weather and temperature. What is your favorite season and temperature? What do you do in cool weather? What do you like to do in cold weather? You could write about that.*

- Remind children that they can use the charts and writing in the classroom for ideas to spell words.

OBJECTIVES

Children
- write independently

MATERIALS
- journals

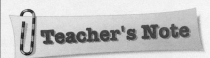

Teacher's Note

Writing ability varies greatly among children in a kindergarten classroom. Encourage children to find words they need on the Word Wall or in decodable books they can read.

Portfolio Opportunity

As children use up their journals, keep the completed ones in their portfolios. Children will be amazed to look back at their earlier work and see how much they've learned.

DAY 5

Literature for Week 2

Different texts for different purposes

The Enormous Turnip

Teacher Read Aloud

Purposes

- oral language
- listening strategy
- comprehension skill

Big Books:

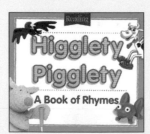

Higglety Pigglety: A Book of Rhymes

Purposes

- oral language development
- phonemic awareness

From Apples to Zebras: A Book of ABC's

Purposes

- alphabet recognition
- letters and sounds

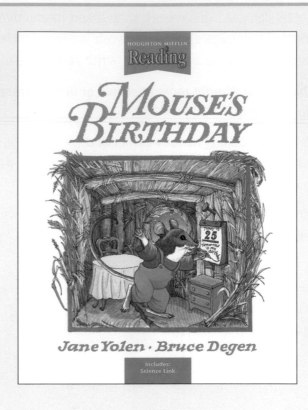

Big Book: Main Selection

Purposes

- concepts of print
- reading strategy
- story language
- comprehension skills

Also available in Little Big Book and audiotape

Also in the Big Book:
- Science Link

Purposes

- reading strategies
- comprehension skills
- concepts of print

Phonics Library

Also available in Take-Home version

Purposes

- applying phonics skills and high-frequency words

Leveled Books

On My Way Practice Reader

To Fan Fox
by *Anne Myers*
page T153

Little Readers for Guided Reading
Collection K

Houghton Mifflin Classroom Bookshelf
Level K

Technology

www.eduplace.com

Log on to *Education Place* for more activities relating to *Down on the Farm*.

www.bookadventure.org

This free Internet reading incentive program provides thousands of titles for students to read.

Instructional Goals

Learning to Read

☑ **Phonemic Awareness:** Blending Phonemes

Strategy Focus: Question

☑ **Comprehension Skill:** Noting Important Details

☑ **Phonics Skills**

Phonemic Awareness: Ending Sound /x/ Final Consonant x; Short o + x

Compare and Review: Initial Consonants: x, t, g

☑ **High-Frequency Word:** the

☑ **Concepts of Print:** Directionality: Return to Sweep; Use of All Capital Letters

Word Work

High-Frequency Word Practice: Word Families: -ox, -ot, -ig

Writing & Language

Vocabulary Skills: Using Exact Naming Words, Using Comparisons

Writing Skills: Writing a Friendly Letter, Using Naming Words

☑ = tested skills

Leveled Books

Have children read in appropriate levels daily.

Phonics Library
On My Way Practice Readers
Little Big Books
Houghton Mifflin Classroom Bookshelf

Day 1

Opening Routines, *T60–T61*

Word Wall
- **Phonemic Awareness:** Blending Phonemes

Teacher Read Aloud
A Classic Russian Folktale, T62–T65
- **Strategy:** Question
- **Comprehension:** Noting Important Details

Phonics

Instruction
- Phonemic Awareness, Ending Sound /x/, *T66–T67; Practice Book, 235–236*

High-Frequency Word Practice
- Words: *a, and, I, is, like, to, T68*

Oral Language
- Using Exact Naming Words, *T69*
- Viewing, Listening, and Speaking, *T69*

Managing Small Groups
Teacher-Led Group
- Reread familiar **Phonics Library** selections

Independent Groups
- Finish *Practice Book, 233–236*
- *Phonics Center:* Theme 8, Week 2, Day 1
- Book, Dramatic Play, other Centers

Day 2

Opening Routines, *T70–T71*

Word Wall
- **Phonemic Awareness:** Blending Phonemes

Sharing the Big Book
Mouse's Birthday, T72–T73
- **Strategy:** Question
- **Comprehension:** Noting Important Details

Phonics

Instruction, Practice
- Final Consonant x, *T74–T75*
- *Practice Book, 237*

High-Frequency Word
- New Word: *the, T76–T77*
- *Practice Book, 238*

High-Frequency Word Practice
- Building Sentences, *T78*

Vocabulary Expansion
- Using Comparisons, *T79*

Managing Small Groups
Teacher-Led Group
- Begin *Practice Book, 237–238* and handwriting **Blackline Masters 180 or 206.**

Independent Groups
- Finish *Practice Book, 237–238* and handwriting **Blackline Masters 180 or 206.**
- *Phonics Center:* Theme 8, Week 2, Day 2
- Art, Writing, other Centers

Technology

Lesson Planner CD-ROM: Customize your planning for *Down on the Farm* with the Lesson Planner.

Day 3

Opening Routines, *T80–T81*

Word Wall
- **Phonemic Awareness:** Blending Phonemes

Sharing the Big Book
Mouse's Birthday, T82–T86
- **Strategy:** Question
- **Comprehension:** Noting Important Details, *T83; Practice Book, 239*
- **Concepts of Print:** Directionality: Return Sweep, *T83;* Use of All Capital Letters, *T85*

Phonics

Practice, Application
- Consonant *x, T88–T89*

Instruction
- Blending *b -ox, T88–T89; Practice Book, 240*
- **Phonics Library:** "The Big, Big Box," *T89*

Building Words
- Word Family: *-ox, T90*

✎ **Shared Writing**
- Writing a Friendly Letter, *T91*

Managing Small Groups
Teacher-Led Group
- Read **Phonics Library** "The Big, Big Box"
- Write letters *O, o;* begin **Blackline Masters 171 or 197.**
- Begin *Practice Book, 239–240*

Independent Groups
- Finish **Blackline Masters 171 or 197** and *Practice Book, 239–240.*
- Art, other Centers

Day 4

Opening Routines, *T92–T93*

Word Wall
- **Phonemic Awareness:** Blending Phonemes

Sharing the Big Book
Science Link: "Who Lives on the Farm?," *T94–T95*
- **Strategy:** Question
- **Comprehension:** Noting Important Details
- **Concepts of Print:** Directionality: Left to Right

Phonics

Practice
- Blending *-ox* Words, *T96–T97; Practice Book, 241*

Building Words
- Word Families: *-ox, -ot, -ig, T98*

✎ **Interactive Writing**
- Using Naming Words, *T99*
- Speaking and Writing, *T99*

Managing Small Groups
Teacher-Led Group
- Reread **Phonics Library** selection "The Big, Big Box"
- Begin *Practice Book, 241*

Independent Groups
- Finish *Practice Book, 241*
- **Phonics Center:** Theme 8, Week 2, Day 4
- Centers

Day 5

Opening Routines, *T100–T101*

Word Wall
- **Phonemic Awareness:** Blending Phonemes

Revisiting the Literature
Comprehension: Noting Important Details, *T102*
Building Fluency
- **Phonics Library:** "The Big, Big Box," *T103*

Phonics

Review
- Familiar Consonants; *-ox, -ot, -ig, T104*

High-Frequency Word Review
- Words: *I, see, my, like, a, to, and, go, is, here, for, have, said, T105; Practice Book, 242*

Building Words
- Word Families: *-ox, -ot, -ig, T106*

✎ **Independent Writing**
- Journals: Independent Writing, *T107*

Managing Small Groups
Teacher-Led Group
- Reread familiar **Phonics Library** selections
- Begin *Practice Book, 242,* **Blackline Master 36.**

Independent Groups
- Reread **Phonics Library** selections
- Finish *Practice Book, 242,* **Blackline Master 36.**
- Centers

Setting up the Centers

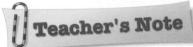

Management Tip Some children who have not lived in a rural environment may need support to help them build background about farms and farm animals. Cut out and paste pictures of animals on index cards for children to name and sort.

Phonics Center

Materials • Phonics Center materials for Theme 8, Week 2

Children work with letters and their sounds this week. They listen for words with final *x, t,* and *g.* They make words with initial consonants *b, f* and the word family - *ox.* Prepare materials for the Day 1, 2 and 4 activities. Cut apart the letter/picture grids and bag them in plastic by color. Put out the Workmats and open the Direction Chart to the appropriate day. Follow the Phonics Center Routine. See pages T67, T75, and T97 for this week's Phonics Center activities.

Book Center

Materials • books about farms and farm machinery

Take the children to the school library and choose a few books to read aloud this week. Look for books about farm machinery. If you have toy or model farm animals, tractors, or other farm equipment, use them to enliven the display.

Writing Center

Materials • crayons • markers • lined and unlined paper

After sharing *Quick as a Cricket* by Audrey and Don Wood, children draw and label similes, such as "quiet as a mouse." See page T58 for this week's Writing Center activity.

Art Center

Materials • crayons or paints • cardboard mouse shapes
• clean, empty milk cartons

As a follow-up to *Mouse's Birthday,* children draw pictures of gifts they would bring to the birthday party. They also make models of mouse houses. Because this activity extends from a discussion of size, supply several sizes of cartons if that is possible. See pages T73 and T87 for this week's Art Center activities.

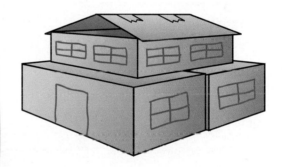

Dramatic Play Center

Materials • Blackline Masters 120–122

Children color the masks from **Blackline Masters 120–122** and reenact the story *The Enormous Turnip.* They will need a narrator for the performance. If you can, make flannel board pieces that children can use to retell the story. See page T63 for this week's Dramatic Play Center activity.

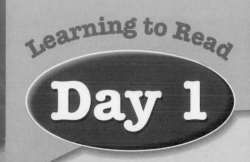

Learning to Read
Day 1

Day at a Glance

Learning to Read

Read Aloud:

The Enormous Turnip

✓ Learning About / ks /, page T66

Word Work

✓ High-Frequency Word Practice, page T68

Writing & Language

Oral Language, *page T69*

 Half-Day Kindergarten

✓ Indicates lessons for tested skills. Choose additional activities as time allows.

Opening

Calendar

Sunday	Monday	Tuesday	Wednesday	Thursday	Friday	Saturday
		1	2	3	4	
5	6	7	8	9	10	11
12	13	14	15	16	17	18
19	20	21	22	23	24	25
26	27	28	29	30	31	

calm

breezy

windy

Help children find today's date on the calendar, and name it for them. Explain that they will be talking about the wind this week. Use a small flag as a wind gauge and show children how to tell if it's calm, breezy, or windy.

Daily Message

Modeled Writing Write a sentence about the day and wind conditions.

Today is Monday.
It is windy.

Have children chant the spelling of each word on the wall today: **I** *spells* **I** *and* s-a-i-d *spells* said *and* m-y *spells* my *and* p-o-t *spells* pot.

Routines

Daily Phonemic Awareness
Blending Phonemes

- Read "Higglety, Pigglety, Pop!" on page 34. Then play a guessing game.

Four Square Sounds Give each child a blank paper and have children fold their papers into four sections.

- *Listen carefully. I'm going to say a word from the poem. When you know it, draw a picture of it in just one square. It doesn't have to be a fancy picture, just enough to tell what you've drawn.*

- Then orally segment /d/ /o/ /g/; /m/ /o/ /p/; (dog, mop). Add /p/ /i/ /g/ and /t/ /o/ /p/ (pig, top). For each word, children tell the answer and display their drawings.

HIGGLETY, PIGGLETY, POP!

Higglety, pigglety, pop!
The dog has eaten the mop.
The pig's in a hurry,
The cat's in a flurry,
Higglety, pigglety, pop!

by Samuel Goodrich

34

Higglety Pigglety: A Book of Rhymes, page 34

Getting Ready to Learn

To help plan their day, tell children that they will

- listen to a story called *The Enormous Turnip.*

- meet a new Alphafriend, Mr. X-Ray.

- act out *The Enormous Turnip* in the Dramatic Play Center.

Learning to Read

Day 1

Read Aloud

Purposes • oral language • listening strategy
• comprehension skill

Selection Summary
A farmer grows a turnip so large that he can't pull it up even with the help of his wife, granddaughter, cat, and dog. Finally, a mouse agrees to help, and together they pull up the turnip.

Key Concept
Teamwork

 English Language Learners

Review vocabulary for family members and pets. Then name a few vegetables and have learners classify them. Talk about the parts of a plant that grow above and below ground.

Teacher Read Aloud
Oral Language/Comprehension

▶ ### Building Background

Tell children that they'll hear a story called *The Enormous Turnip*. If children have ever tasted a turnip, have them describe it. If possible, bring in or show a picture of a turnip.

Talk about the meaning of *enormous*. **Show with your hands the meaning of** little, big, **and** enormous! *If something is enormous, is it big or little? How big? Show us.*

Strategy: Question

Teacher Modeling Model the Question Strategy as you read the title and show the illustration.

 Think Aloud

If I don't understand something that happens in a story, I can ask myself a question. That may help. The answer might be in the words or in the pictures.

Comprehension Focus: Noting Important Details

Teacher Modeling Remind children that as you read, you'll think about important things that happen in the story. That will help you understand the story better.

Think Aloud

I'll pay special attention to the things that happen. This helps me know more about the characters and about what happens in the story. You listen and do that too.

▶ Listening to the Story

Read the story aloud, emphasizing the repetitive story language. Children will enjoy chiming in when they can. Note that the Read Aloud art also appears on the back of the Theme Poster.

▶ Responding

Retelling the Story Help children summarize the story with these prompts:

Overset from main column

- *Why was the turnip so hard to pull up?*

- *Who helped the farmer pull the enormous turnip?*

- *Which animal helped at the very end?*

Practice Book pages 233–234 Children will complete the pages during small group time.

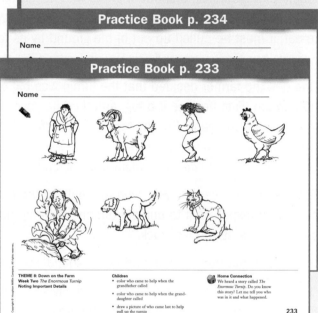

Practice Book p. 234

Practice Book p. 233

At Group Time

Dramatic Play Center

Duplicate and cut several copies of **Blackline Master 120–122** for the Art Center. Have children color the characters. They use the characters to retell or re-enact the story.

📎 Teacher's Note

On a subsequent reading, add pictures of characters to a flannel board as they're mentioned in this story. See **Blackline Masters 120–122** for patterns.

The Enormous Turnip

A Classic Russian Folktale

Once upon a time, a farmer planted a turnip seed, and this is what he said to it, "Grow, turnip, grow! Grow big, and grow strong!"

The turnip heard, and it did. It grew into a big, huge, enormous turnip. In fact, some who saw it say it was the biggest, strongest turnip in the land.

Now as you may know, or as you may not know, a turnip is a vegetable that grows like a carrot. It grows with its leaves sticking up out of the ground and the eating part under the ground. When it is ready to eat, it must be pulled up out of the ground by its top. **(Say:** *Knowing how turnips grow will help you understand the story better.*)

One day, the farmer decided that the turnip was big enough to pull up and eat. First he gave it a tug, and then he gave it a pull, and then he gave it a yank. But the turnip stayed stuck in the ground. **(Ask:** *Why do you think the farmer couldn't pull the turnip out of the ground? What can he do now? What would you do?***)**

The man then called his wife, who was milking the cow. "Wife, please come and help. I want to pull our enormous turnip out of the ground so we can eat it, but it's stuck."

The woman put her arms around her husband's waist and held fast.

"One, two, three!" they said together and gave a mighty pull. But the turnip didn't budge from its place in the ground.

So the woman called their granddaughter, who was feeding the chickens, "Granddaughter, please come and help! We want to pull our enormous turnip out of the ground so we can eat it, but it's stuck!"

The granddaughter put her arms around the woman who held fast to her husband who held on to the top of the turnip. "One, two, three!" they said together and pulled as hard as they could. But the turnip was still stuck in the ground.

Then the granddaughter called the black dog that was sleeping in the sun, "Black dog, please come and help! We want to pull our enormous turnip out of the ground so we can eat it, but it's stuck. **(Ask:** *How do they think a dog could help? Will they get the turnip out? Why do you think so?***)**

The black dog grabbed the coat of the girl who held onto the woman, who held fast to her husband, who held on to the top of the turnip. "One, two, three," they said together and pulled as hard as they could. But the turnip was still stuck in the ground.

Now the black dog called the orange cat that was sitting in a tree. "Orange cat, please come and help! We want to pull our enormous turnip out of the ground so we can eat it, but it's stuck!"

This time on the count of three, the cat pulled the dog's tail, who pulled on the coat of the girl, who pulled on the woman, who held fast to her husband, who held on to the top of the turnip. They all pulled as hard as they could. But the turnip was still stuck in the ground!

Finally the orange cat called a tiny little mouse that was watching from a safe distance. **(Ask:** *A mouse? Do you think a little mouse could be much help getting the enormous turnip unstuck? Why?***)** "Oh, little mouse, please come and help! We want to pull our enormous turnip out of the ground so we can eat it, but it's stuck!"

"Do you promise you won't eat me?" asked the tiny little mouse.

"We promise," said the rest.

So the mouse pulled on the cat's tail, who pulled on the dog's tail, who pulled on the coat of the girl, who pulled on the woman, who held fast to her husband, who held on to the top of the turnip. They all pulled as hard as they could.

"One, two, three!" they counted together and pulled as hard as they could. And guess what! OUT CAME THE TURNIP with a loud "POP!"

"Hurrah!" they all cheered.

The woman then cooked the enormous turnip for her family, and she even gave a bit of it to all the animals who helped. But she saved the sweetest part for the little mouse.

(Ask: *Do you think it was the mouse that finally made the turnip come out of the ground? What do you think happened?***)**

Day 1

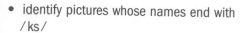
Children

- identify pictures whose names end with /ks/

MATERIALS

- **Alphafriend Cards** Gertie Goose, Tiggy Tiger, Mr. X-Ray
- **Alphafriend Audiotape** Theme 8
- **Alphafolder** Mr. X-Ray
- **Picture Cards** box, bug, fox, hat, ox, six
- **Phonics Center:** Theme 8, Week 2, Day 1

Phonemic Awareness
✓ Final Sound

▶ Introducing the Alphafriend: Mr. X-Ray

Use the Alphafriend routine to introduce Mr. X-Ray.

1 **Alphafriend Riddle** Read these clues. Tell children to listen for the sound at the *end* of the words:

- *This Alphafriend's sound is /ks/. It's really two sounds blended together. Listen again: /ks/. Say it with me: /ks/.*

- *This Alphafriend is a special kind of picture. This picture lets you see inside you—it's a picture of your bones.*

- *Listen: It can show the inside bones of an ox or a fox.*

When most hands are up, call on a child to guess *x-ray*.

2 **Pocket Chart** Display Mr. X-Ray in a pocket chart. Say his name, emphasizing the /ks/ sound slightly, and have children echo this.

3 🎞 **Alphafriend Audiotape** Play Mr. X-Ray's song. *Listen for the /ks/ sound.*

4 **Alphafolder** Have children name the /ks/ pictures in the illustration.

5 **Summarize**

- *What is our Alphafriend's name? What is his sound?*

- *Each time you look at Mr. X-Ray this week, remember the /ks/ sound.*

Mr. X-Ray's Song

Look at Mr. X-Ray.
   What do you see?
I see Mr. X-Ray
   smiling at me.
X is for x-ray that I
   spy.
X comes before the
   letter Y.

🏠 Home Connection

A take-home version of the Mr. X-Ray's song is on an **Alphafriend Blackline Master.** Children can share the song with their families.

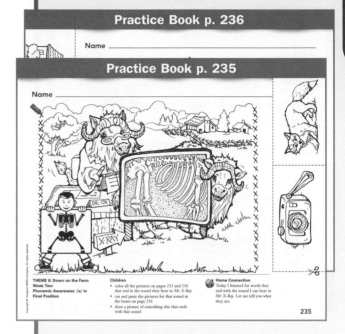

▶ Listening for /ks/

Compare and Review: /ks/, /t/, /g/ Display Alphafriends *Mr. X-Ray, Tiggy Tiger,* and *Gertie Goose.* Review each character's sound.

Hold up the Picture Cards one at a time. Remind children to listen for Mr. X-Ray's sound. Say each picture name twice, emphasizing the final sound. Tell children to signal "thumbs up" for pictures that end with Mr. X-Ray's sound, /ks/. Put the cards below Mr. X-Ray's picture. Emphasize that children are listening for the sound at the end of the word. (Pictures: *six, fox, box, ox, hat, bug*)

Tell children that they will sort more pictures in the Phonics Center today.

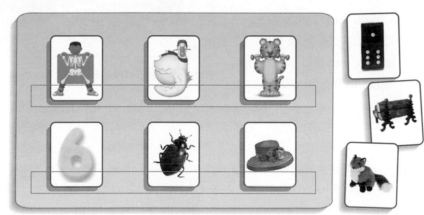

▶ Apply

Practice Book pages 235–236 Children will complete the pages at small group time.

At Group Time

Phonics Center

Use the Phonics Center materials for **Theme 8, Week 2, Day 1.**

Day 1

OBJECTIVES

Children

- read high-frequency words
- create and write sentences with high-frequency

MATERIALS

- *Higglety Pigglety: A Book of Rhymes,* page 18
- **Word Cards** *a, and, I, is, like, to*
- **Picture Cards** for sentence building
- **Punctuation Card:** period

Portfolio Opportunity

Children may wish to save their pictures in their portfolios.

✓ High-Frequency Word Practice

▶ Matching Words

- Distribute Word Cards *a, and, I, like, is,* and *to.* Choose children to read the words and find their matches on the Word Wall. They exchange cards with others.

- Read "Rainy Day." Children will hold up a card when they hear the word in the poem.

- Children exchange Word Cards again, read the words, and find and match them to the print in the book.

Rainy Day

I do not like a rainy day.
The road is wet, the sky is gray.
They dress me up, from head to toes,
In lots and lots of rubber clothes.
I wish the sun would come and stay.
I do not like a rainy day.

by William Wise

13

Higglety Pigglety: A Book of Rhymes, **page 13**

Writing Opportunity Have children use the high-frequency words they know to write about *The Enormous Turnip.* They can draw and label a picture from the story. Encourage children to use temporary phonics spellings but insist on correct spellings of Word Wall words.

I like a t_____

Oral Language

▶ Using Exact Naming Words

Viewing, Listening, and Speaking Look again at the illustration for *The Enormous Turnip,* on T65. Ask: **Who can name the characters you see? I'll write them down.**

- Read the list aloud. Then tell children that these are naming words.

- Have children close their eyes. Say the word *animal.* After a few minutes of "think time," choose a child to name the animal he or she thought of. Write the answer. Ask: **Did someone have a different idea?** Write all the ideas children offer.

- *Now suppose I had said* cow. *Would you know exactly the animal I was thinking about?*

- *Let's try again. Close your eyes and think of a* building. *Tell me all the buildings you thought of. Now, suppose I say* barn. *How does that help?*

- Tell children that authors use exact naming words to help readers know just what they are thinking.

OBJECTIVES ◎

Children
- recognize exact naming words

 English Language Learners

Remind learners of the difference between general naming words and exact (specific) naming words. Recall exact naming words from *The Enormous Turnip.* Then have children think of a general naming word that could contain each. For example: animals would be the umbrella term for *dog, cat, mouse.*

Day at a Glance

Learning to Read

Big Book:

Mouse's Birthday

☑ **Phonics:** Final Consonant *x*, *page T74*

☑ **High- Frequency Word:** *the*, *page T76*

Word Work

High-Frequency Word Practice, *page T78*

Writing & Language

Vocabulary Expansion, *page T79*

 Half-Day Kindergarten

☑ Indicates lessons for tested skills. Choose additional activities as time allows.

Opening

Calendar

Sunday	Monday	Tuesday	Wednesday	Thursday	Friday	Saturday
			1	2	3	4
5	6	7	8	9	10	11
12	13	14	15	16	17	18
19	20	21	22	23	24	25
26	27	28	29	30	31	

Help children find and name today's date. Check your wind flag and have children identify the day as calm, breezy, or windy, and add the appropriate symbol to the calendar.

Daily Message

Modeled Writing Write about something children will do today.

> We will read a new book today.
>
> It's called <u>Mouse's Birthday.</u>

Play "Pass the Pointer." Name a word and pass the pointer to a child. That child finds the word on the wall and names another word. Then he or she passes the pointer to a friend.

Routines

 ## Daily Phonemic Awareness
Blending Phonemes

Tell children that you have a barn full of "secret" farm animals that you need help identifying so that you can put them away. Hold the Picture Cards on your lap, face down. Pick up the top card, holding it so that children can't see the picture.

Say the word, segmenting it by phonemes: /h/ /e/ /n/. Repeat the phonemes, giving children time to think and blend. When children blend the phonemes correctly and say the word *hen,* hold up the Picture Card so they can check their responses.

Do the same for these groups of phonemes: /g/ /oa/ /t/ (goat); /p/ /i/ /g/ (pig); /c/ /ow/ (cow); /o/ /x/ (ox).

Getting Ready to Learn

To help plan their day, tell children that they will

- listen to a Big Book: *Mouse's Birthday.*

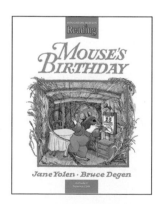

- Learn the new letters *X* and *x* and see words that end with *x.*

- act out the story of *Mouse's Birthday* in the Dramatic Play Center.

gift

Day 2

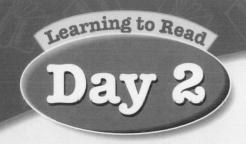

HOUGHTON MIFFLIN
Reading

MOUSE'S BIRTHDAY

Jane Yolen · Bruce Degen

Includes:
Science Link

Purposes • concepts of print • story language
• reading strategy • comprehension skill

Selection Summary
This rhythmic, rhyming tale tells how Mouse's farm friends bring him gifts, expanding his tiny home beyond its capacity. After the house bursts open, Mouse gets the best gift of all—a new home, big enough for all his friends.

Key Concepts
Size
Farm animals

Sharing the Big Book
Oral Language/Comprehension

▶ Building Background

Introduce the Big Book by reading the title and the names of the author and the illustrator. Talk about birthdays children have celebrated. How might a farm mouse's birthday be different from their own? Talk about the sizes of a variety of farm animals. Ask children to show with their hands the size of a mouse, a cat, a cow, and a farmer. Then have the group predict what the book will be about.

Strategy: Question

Teacher Modeling Model the Question Strategy as you read the title and point to the pictures.

> **Think Aloud**
>
> *As I read, sometimes I find it helpful to ask myself questions about the book. When I'm finished, I can see if my questions were answered. For this book, I'll ask: Who helps Mouse celebrate his birthday? Do they all fit in his house? Let's see if we can find the answers as we read.*

Comprehension Focus:
Noting Important Details

Teacher Modeling Model how to note important details as you read.

> **Think Aloud**
>
> *Another thing that helps me when I read is keeping track of important things that happen. As we read, let's look and listen carefully for parts of the story that may be important. This will help us understand the story better and figure out what may happen next.*

▶ Sharing the Story

Read the selection aloud, emphasizing its rhyme and rhythm. Track the print with a pointer or your finger as you read. Pause often to invite children to supply repetitive text or a rhyming word.

▶ Responding

Personal Response Ask children what they liked best about this story. If they could speak with Jane Yolen, the author, what would they tell her? Then help children summarize the story, using these prompts:

- *Who came to Mouse's party? Let's look in the book to help us remember.*

- *What gifts did Mouse get? Which gift did you like best? What gift would you have taken him?*

- *What happened when Mouse blew out the candle on his cake?*

- *Would you like to go to Mouse's birthday party?*

- *What animals would you invite to a party if you were Mouse?*

At Group Time

Art Center

At the Art Center, have children draw and label gifts they would bring if they had been invited to Mouse's birthday. Save the drawings for a later activity.

MEETING INDIVIDUAL NEEDS **English Language Learners**

Talk about things usually associated with a birthday party (cake, candles, balloons, presents, food) and show pictures of these objects. Take a picture walk and help learners describe what they see. Point to the size of Mouse's guests. Encourage children to talk about the differences.

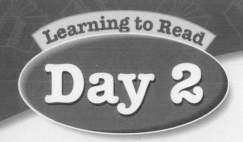

Extra Support

To help children remember the letter sounds, remind them that sometimes the letter's name gives a clue to its sound: *x,* /ks/. Also, the Alphafriend *Mr. X-Ray* is shaped like the letter *x*.

Phonics

✔ Final Consonant x

▶ Develop Phonemic Awareness

Beginning/Ending Sounds Play Mr. X-Ray's Song, and have children sing along. Have them listen for the /ks/ sound. Tell them to say /ks/ and cross their arms over their chests for each /ks/ word they hear.

> **Mr. X-Ray's Song**
> (tune: "Hush, Little Baby")
> Look at Mr. X-Ray.
>   What do you see?
> I see Mr. X-Ray
>   smiling at me.
> X is for x-ray that I
>   spy.
> X comes before the
>   letter Y.

▶ Connect Sounds to Letters

Final Letter Display the *Mr. X-Ray* card, and have children name the letter on the picture. Say: *The letter* x *stands for the sound* /ks/, *as in* x-ray. *But very few words begin with* x. *You will usually see the letter* x *at the end of a word, such as* box. *When you see an* x, *remember* Mr. X-Ray *and* box. *That will help you remember the sound* /ks/.

Compare and Review: *x, t, g* In a pocket chart, display the Picture and Letter Cards as shown. Review the sounds for final /t/ and /g/. Then hold up the picture cards, one at a time. Ask: *Do you hear Mr. X-Ray's sound* /ks/? *Where do you hear it?* Display the remaining Picture Cards in random order. Children can name a picture, say the end sound, and put the card below the letter that stands for the end sound in the picture name.

▶ Handwriting

Writing X, x Tell children that now they'll learn to write the letters that stand for /ks/: capital *X* and small *x*. Write each letter as you recite the handwriting rhyme. Children can chant each rhyme as they "write" the letter in the air.

Handwriting Rhyme: X

Tall line leans
like a slanted stick.
Another line crosses
quick, quick, quick.

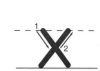

Handwriting Rhyme: x

Little x isn't
hard to do.
The first one slants
and the other one too.

▶ Apply

Practice Book page 237 Children will complete the page at small group time.

Blackline Master 180 This page provides additional handwriting practice for small group time.

DAY 2

Practice Book p. 237

At Group Time

Phonics Center

Use the Phonics Center materials for **Theme 8, Week 2, Day 2.**

✓ High-Frequency Word
New Word: the

▶ Teach

Tell children that today they'll learn a new word. It's a very useful word because they'll see it often in books. They also use it when they speak. Say *the* and use it in context.

The cows said, "Moo."   A farmer fed *the* pigs.   I rode *the* horse.

Write *the* on the board, and have children spell it as you point to the letters. Say, **Spell the *with me:* t-h-e,** /the/. Then lead children in a chant, clapping on each beat, to help them remember the letters in *the*: **t-h-e, *the!* t-h-e, *the!***

Word Wall Post *the* on the Word Wall, and remind children to look there when they need to remember how to write the word.

▶ Practice

Reading Demonstrate the fact that children will encounter the word *the* frequently by holding up Little Big Books whose titles contain it. Children read the word and notice whether it has a capital or small form.

Build sentences in a pocket chart. Children can take turns reading. Display the chart as a guide for children to practice reading the sentences.

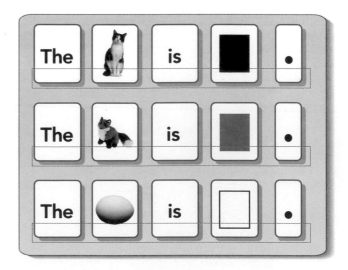

Display *Higglety Pigglety: A Book of Rhymes,* page 27.

- Share the poem "The Itsy Bitsy Spider" aloud.

- Reread the poem slowly, tracking the print. Have children point to the word *the* when it appears.

The Itsy Bitsy Spider

The itsy bitsy spider
Climbed up the waterspout.

Down came the rain
And washed the spider out.

Out came the sun
And dried up all the rain,

And the itsy bitsy spider
Climbed up the spout again.

27

Higglety Pigglety: A Book of Rhymes, page 27

▶ Apply

Practice Book page 238 Children will read and write *the* as they complete the Practice Book page. They will practice reading *the* in the **Phonics Library** story "The Big, Big Box."

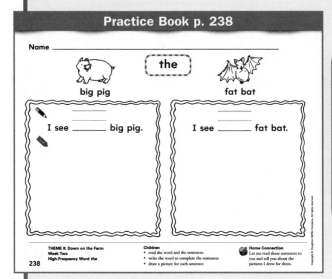

Practice Book p. 238

Name _____

big pig   the   fat bat

I see _____ big pig.   I see _____ fat bat.

238

THEME 8: Down on the Farm
Week Two
High-Frequency Word *the*

Children
- read the word and the sentences
- write the word to complete the sentences
- draw a picture for each sentence

Home Connection
Let me read these sentences to you and tell you about the pictures I drew for them.

Diagnostic Check

If . . .	You can . . .
children don't readily recognize *the* on the Practice Book page,	have them make the word with magnetic letters and use it in oral sentences.

High-Frequency Words   T77

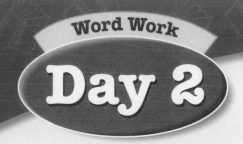

High-Frequency Word Practice

▶ Building Sentences

Tell children that they'll write about a farm animal. Display Word Cards and Picture Cards for *horse, pig,* and *hen* and choose a child to decide which one to write about. Make word cards for *ran* and *man* and display them with the Word Cards *The, the* and *to.*

■ *Let's start our sentence with our new word,* the. *Who can find* the *for us? That's right! But wait! There are two cards for* the! *Which one should we use—the one that begins with capital* T *or small* t? *How do you know?*

Build this sentence, helping children notice that *The* and *the* are the same word. Stress that capital letters appear at the beginning of sentences.

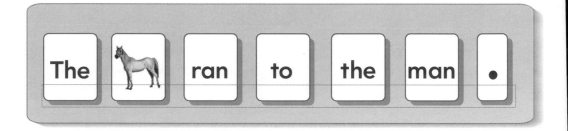

■ Read the sentence together. Let children substitute different pictures and practice reading more sentences.

Writing Opportunity Have children write sentences like the one you built together, choosing different farm animals to complete them. Children can draw and label their stories.

Vocabulary Expansion

▶ Using Comparisons

■ Browse through *Mouse's Birthday* again. Ask: *How big was Mouse's house?*

■ Tell children that one good way to describe something is to compare it with something else. *I could say this: Mouse's house is as small as a baby's shoe. How big is a baby's shoe? Show me with your fingers. What else would show how small it is?*

Continue with these comparisons.

As tall as _____.   As quiet as _____.

As loud as _____.   As enormous as _____.

As huge as _____.   As tasty as _____.

As hard as _____.   As neat as _____.

As tiny as _____.

DAY 2

At Group Time
Writing Center

Feature *Quick as a Cricket,* by Audrey and Don Wood, as a Read Aloud and in your Book Corner. This book is a great one to reinforce and extend the comparisons children have been making. Then in the Writing Center, children draw comparisons such as *as quiet as a mouse.*

MEETING INDIVIDUAL NEEDS
English Language Learners

Learners may have trouble with the abstract nature of comparisons. To help, provide real objects or pictures of concrete objects to which things are compared. For example, show a rock and a thimble to explain these comparisons: *as hard as a rock, as tiny as a thimble.*

Day 3

Day at a Glance

Learning to Read

Big Book:

Mouse's Birthday

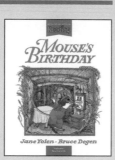

 Phonics:
Blending b -ox,
page T88

Word Work

Building Words, *page T90*

Writing & Language

Shared Writing, *page T91*

 Half-Day Kindergarten

☑ Indicates lessons for tested skills. Choose additional activities as time allows.

Opening

Calendar

Sunday	Monday	Tuesday	Wednesday	Thursday	Friday	Saturday
		1	2	3	4	
5	6	7	8	9	10	11
12	13	14	15	16	17	18
19	20	21	22	23	24	25
26	27	28	29	30	31	

Help children find and name today's date. Check your wind flag and have children identify the day as calm, breezy, or windy. Add the appropriate symbol to the calendar.

 calm breezy windy

Daily Message

Modeled Writing Use the name of the month in the message. Ask children to spell the word as you point to it.

This is (March).
March is a
windy month.

 Word Wall

Choose volunteers to read words that have only one letter each: *I* and *a.* Continue with two- and three-letter words. Tell children that some words are short and some are longer. This can help them recognize and read these words.

✓ Daily Phonemic Awareness
Blending Phonemes

- Read "The Picnic" on page 37 in the *Higglety Pigglety: A Book of Rhymes.*

- Play a guessing game.

- *I'll read a line from the poem. Then I'll say the sounds from one of the words in that line, and you guess the word.*

- Read the first line from the poem. Then say: */r/ /u/ /g/. What word has these sounds: /r/ /u/ /g/?* (rug)

- Continue the game with other lines from the poem, helping children blend the phonemes for *box* (/b/ /o/ /x/), *up* (/u/ /p/), and *fun* (/f/ /u/ /n/).

The Picnic

We brought a rug for sitting on,
Our lunch was in a box.
The sand was warm. We didn't wear
Hats or shoes or socks.

Waves came curling up the beach.
We waded. It was fun.
Our sandwiches were different kinds.
I dropped my jelly one.

by Dorothy Aldis

Higglety Pigglety: A Book of Rhymes, page 37

Getting Ready to Learn

To help plan their day, tell children that they will

- reread and talk about the Big Book *Mouse's Birthday.*

- read a story called "The Big, Big Box."

- build a Mouse House in the Art Center.

DAY 3

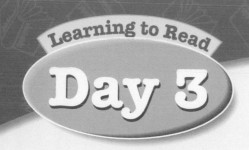

Sharing the Big Book

OBJECTIVES

Children

- note important details
- identify directionality in print
- recognize the use of all capital letters

Big Book

MOUSE'S BIRTHDAY

Jane Yolen · Bruce Degen

Reading for Understanding Reread the story, encouraging children to have fun with the rhyme and the humor of the book. Pause for Supporting Comprehension points.

 Extra Support

Reread Mouse's Birthday with a small group. Help them focus on details in the art that help explain what happens.

MOUSE'S BIRTHDAY

Jane Yolen
ILLUSTRATED BY
Bruce Degen

HOUGHTON MIFFLIN   BOSTON · MORRIS PLAINS, NJ
California · Colorado · Georgia · Illinois · New Jersey · Texas

Mouse's house is very small,

1

title page, page 1

Very small,

Very small,

2

3

pages 2–3

Hardly any room at all
For anyone but Mouse.

4

5

pages 4–5

In comes Cat upon his knees,
Carrying a gift of cheese,
Trying very hard to squeeze
Into Mouse's house.

pages 6–7

In comes Dog upon his knees,
Carrying a pot of teas,
Trying very hard to squeeze
Into Mouse's house.

pages 8–9

In comes Cow upon her knees,
Carrying a bowl of peas,
Trying very hard to squeeze
Into Mouse's house.

pages 10–11

▶ Supporting Comprehension

title page

Strategy: Question

Teacher-Student Modeling Review how to form questions before reading and how to answer them after reading. Prompts:

■ *What questions did we have about the story? What were we curious about? How did the story and pictures answer these questions?*

page 1

Comprehension Focus: Noting Details

Teacher-Student Modeling Remind children that pictures often contain important information that will help them understand a story. Prompts:

■ *Look closely at Mouse's house. Where is it? How can you tell?* (It's in a haystack inside a barn; we can tell by the walls and beams around the outside.) *Why is knowing this important to understanding the story?*

pages 6–11

Making Inferences

■ *Why do Cat and Cow come in on their knees?*
(Because of their size; they are too big for Mouse's door.)

Revisiting the Text

page 4

Concepts of Print

 Directionality: Return Sweep

■ Track the print as you reread the selection. On page 4, pause after the word *all*, and say, *After I read this word, which word will I read next?* (*For*) Exaggerate the return sweep with your hand and arm, and then continue reading the page.

DAY 3

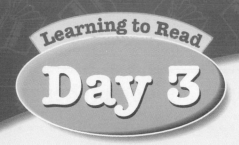

▶ Supporting Comprehension

pages 12–13

Fantasy/Realism

■ *Do you think a horse could really fit into a mouse's house? What does this tell you about this story? Could it really happen?* (A horse couldn't fit; it is a made-up story.)

pages 14–15

Making Judgments

■ *Look at the size of Mouse's presents. Do they seem to be the right size for him?*

---

pages 12–13

✓ Comprehension Focus: Noting Details

Teacher-Student Modeling *Let's think about Mouse's house. Tell me about the size of Mouse's house and what may happen to it. What parts in the pictures and words tell us about the size of Mouse's house? How does this help you figure out what will happen?*

Oral Language

On a rereading, note interesting words.

valise: A valise is a small suitcase. The farmer's valise is brown.

whoosh: A sound word. Invite children to say the word *whoosh* with you, stretching out the *ooo* sound. Help them note that the word sounds like the noise it stands for.

pages 12–13

pages 14–15

pages 16–17

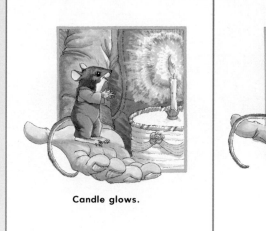 

Candle glows.   Mouse blows.

18   19

pages 18–19

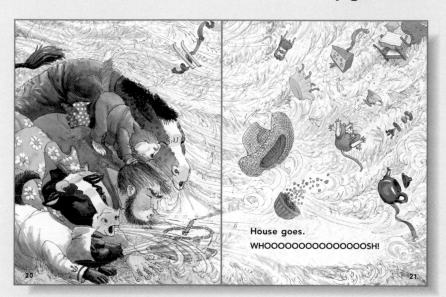

House goes.
WHOOOOOOOOOOOOOOOOSH!

20   21

pages 20–21

23

pages 22–23

▶ **Supporting Comprehension**

pages 18–21

Cause and Effect

■ *Tell about what happened in these pictures. What happened to Mouse's house? Why did this happen?* (Mouse blew out the candle, and his house burst apart. The animals were too big for the house, and blowing out the candle was finally too much for it.)

pages 22–23

Strategy: Question

Teacher-Student Modeling *As I read pages 20 and 21, I asked myself, "Where will the animals end up?" I notice on pages 22 and 23 they are sitting on the floor of the barn. What questions did you ask yourself? What did you wonder about?*

Revisiting the Text

pages 20-21

Concepts of Print

✓ **Use of All Capital Letters**

Point to the word *WHOOOOSH* on page 21. *What kind of voice should I use when I read this word?* (loud, excited) *So what does the author mean when she writes story words in all capital letters?*

MEETING INDIVIDUAL NEEDS **Extra Support**

Help children with the return sweep by having them put their hand on your arm and point with you as you read and track the print.

DAY 3

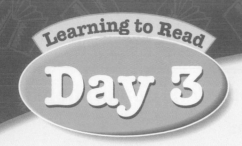
▶ ## Supporting Comprehension

pages 24–26

✓ ### Comprehension Focus: Noting Details

Student Modeling *I notice that Mouse seems very happy in his new house and that he has made it comfortable. How do the pictures help us know this?*

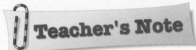
Teacher's Note

Language Patterns

Rhyme Almost every page contains rhyming words. Help children hear and repeat those words.

English Language Learners

Go back through the pages of the story. Call on children to tell what is happening in each picture, to name animals, or to find rhyming words, depending on their level of proficiency. Guide children with a mix of yes-no, multiple-choice, and short-answer questions.

Mouse's **new** house is very wide,
Very wide,
Very wide.
Everyone can fit inside,
Including little Mouse.

pages 24–25

page 26

▶ Responding to the Story

Retelling Use these prompts to help children retell the story:

- *Who came to Mouse's birthday party? What presents did they bring?*

- *What happened when Mouse blew out the candle?*

- *Do you think Mouse will like his new house? Why?*

- *Is there anything you wondered about in the beginning of the story? Did you find the answer? How?*

Practice Book page 239 Children will complete the page at small group time.

Literature Circle Have small groups discuss the presents the animals and the farmer brought and vote on which ones they think Mouse liked most.

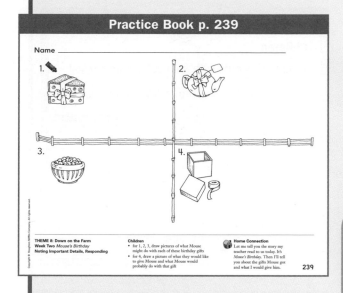

Practice Book p. 239

DAY 3

At Group Time

Art Center

Materials • empty boxes • paints • glue • scissors • cardboard mouse shapes • yarn

Talk about the size of a mouse's house. Have children build a house for a mouse by gluing small boxes together and cutting doors and windows. They can draw mice and use yarn as tails for the mice. Encourage children to re-enact parts of the story, using their mouse houses.

MEETING INDIVIDUAL NEEDS

Challenge

Some children will be ready to match isolated words on cards to ones in the text. Make word cards for some of the rhyming words, putting small picture clues on the cards. Have children match the words and confirm by matching the pictures on their cards to the ones in the book.

Diagnostic Check

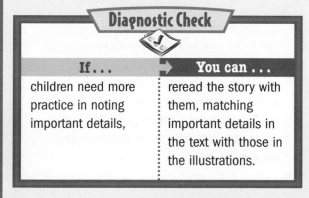

If . . .	You can . . .
children need more practice in noting important details,	reread the story with them, matching important details in the text with those in the illustrations.

Responding T87

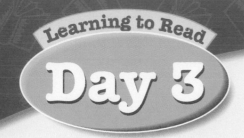
Children

- identify words with final consonant *x*, /ks/
- blend and read words with *b, f,* and *-ox*

MATERIALS

- **Alphafriend Cards** *Ozzie Octopus, Mr. X-Ray*
- **Letter Cards** *b, f, l, o, x*
- **Alphafriend Audiotape** Theme 8

Practice Book p. 240

Name _____

┌─────────────┐
│ fox   box │
└─────────────┘

1. See my _____ ?
   ☺ ☹

2. Is my _____ big?
   ☺ ☹

3. Is it a box for my _____ ?
   ☺ ☹

THEME 8: Down on the Farm
Week Two
Phonics: -ox Words

Children
• read the sentences and write words ending in -er to complete them
• mark the smile (yes) or the frown (no) to show whether the pictures answer the questions

Home Connection
Let me read these questions to you. We can cut out the words at the top into separate letters, scramble them, and build the words again.

240

Provide separate sets of letters to form words, such as: *b-o-x* and *r-u-g*. As you say the phonemes aloud, guide children in putting the letters together and repeating the sounds aloud.

Phonics
✓ *Blending b -ox*

▶ Connect Sounds to Letters

Review Consonant *x* Play Mr. X-Ray's song, and have children clap for each word that ends with /ks/. Write *X* and *x* on the board, and list words from the song. Remind children that they will usually find *x*/ks/ at the end of a word.

Blending *-ox* Tell children that they'll build a word with *x*, but first they'll recall a vowel ("helper letter"). Display Alphafriend *Ozzie Octopus*. **Say Ozzie Octopus with me. Ozzie's letter is the vowel o, and the sound o usually stands for is /ŏ/. You say /ŏ/. Listen for /ŏ/ in these words: /ŏ/ on, /ŏ/ odd, /ŏ/ opposite.**

Hold up the Letter Cards *o* and *x*. Remind children that they know the sound for *x*. Model blending the sounds as you hold the cards apart and then together: **/ŏ/ /ks/, ox. I've made the word ox. Now it's your turn.** Children say the word as you point and blend.

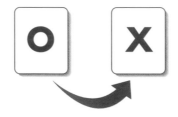

Blending *-ox* Words Then put *b* in front of *ox*, and model blending /b/ /o/ /ks/, *box*. Choose a child to read the word as you point. Continue with *fox, lox*.

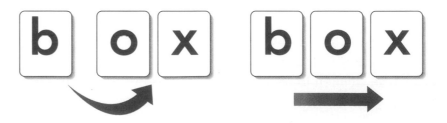

Word Wall Add *box* to the Word Wall. Children will use *box* to remind them how to make other *-ox* words.

Practice Book page 240 Children complete the page at small group time.

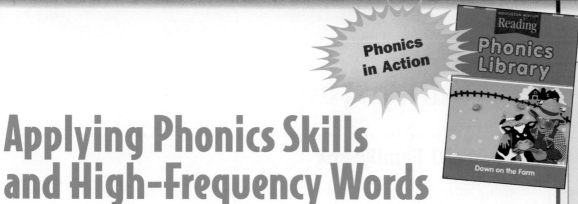

Applying Phonics Skills and High-Frequency Words

Phonics in Action

Phonics/Decoding Strategy

Teacher-Student Modeling Discuss using the Phonics/Decoding Strategy to read the story.

Think Aloud

Here's our new story. You can read it all by yourselves! Let's look at the title. Who can find our new Word Wall word, the? Find the word that belongs to the -ox family. Right. It's Box. Now let's read the whole title together. Point to each word so I'll know you can read it.

▶ Coached Reading

Introduce Fan Fox and Dan Cat, and then have children begin reading quietly along. Because most beginning readers are not yet able to read silently, have them "whisper read." Prompts:

page 9   *What do you think is in the big, big box? Let's find out.*

page 10   *Fan Fox thinks it is her box. Who will read what she says?*

page 11   *Does Dan Cat agree with Fan? How do you know? Read what Dan says.*

page 13   *What do Fan and Dan find in the box?* (a mat and a hat)

page 14   *Do you think the mat will fit? How about the hat? Who will read the questions?*

page 15   *Did the story end happily? How do you know? Now let's read the whole story together. We'll take turns. You point when someone else is reading.*

Phonics Library

Purposes
- apply phonics skills
- apply high-frequency words

The Big, Big Box
by Ann Spivey
illustrated by Gavin Bishop

9

It is a big, big, big box!
"It is my big, big, big box."

10

"It is not," said Dan Cat.
"It is my big, big, big box!"

11

Fan bit it.
Dan hit it.

12

It is a big, big, big mat!
It is a big, big, big hat!

13

Can it fit?
Can it fit?

14

Fan sat.
Dan sat.

15

Home Connection

Children can color the pictures in the take-home version of "The Big, Big Box." After rereading the story on Day 4, they can take it home.

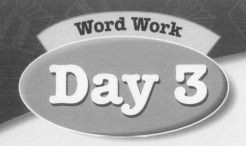

Day 3

OBJECTIVES

Children

- blend initial consonants with -ox to read words

MATERIALS

- **Letter Cards** b, f, l, o, p, x

Building Words

▶ Word Family: -ox

Using letter cards, model how to build *ox.* **Listen: / ŏ /... / ks /. How many sounds do you hear? The first sound is / ŏ /. What do I need to spell that? The last sounds are / ks /. What letter should I choose? Read the word.** (ox) **Now, what letter do I need to write** box? **Read the word. Now what happens if I change / b / to / f /? Read the new word.** Have children use *ox, box,* and *fox* in oral sentences.

Have small groups work together to build *-ox* words. They can use sandpaper letters or other manipulatives in your collection.

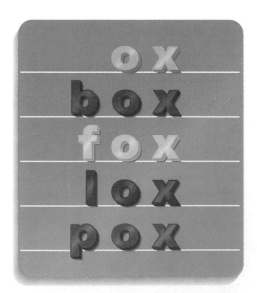

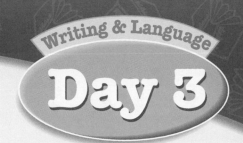
Shared Writing

▶ Writing a Friendly Letter

Use the Big Book to review the gifts Mouse received for his birthday. Talk about ways Mouse might thank his friends. Maybe he'll write them a letter!

■ Share the writing of a letter to the cat, thanking him for the cheese.

■ Model the print conventions.

■ *How do we start a letter? I think Mouse would write* Dear Cat. *Who can tell me how to spell Cat?*

■ *What will we say first? Cat gave Mouse a gift. But if he writes the word* cheese *it will tell exactly what he's thanking his friend for. So let's do that.*

■ Delicious *is a good describing word.*

■ *How will Mouse end the letter?*

■ *Let's read the letter together.*

> Dear Cat,
>   Thank you for the delicious cheese! I'm glad you came to my birthday party.
>   Your friend,
>   Mouse

OBJECTIVES

Children
• share the writing of a class letter

MATERIALS

• **Big Book:** *Mouse's Birthday*

DAY 3

Day 4

Day at a Glance

Learning to Read

Big Book:

Who Lives on the Farm?

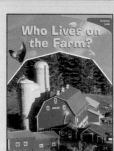

 Phonics: Reviewing /ks/;

Blending *-ox* Words, *page T96*

Word Work

Building Words, *page T98*

Writing & Language

Interactive Writing, *page T99*

Half-Day Kindergarten

 Indicates lessons for tested skills. Choose additional activities as time allows.

Opening

Calendar

Sunday	Monday	Tuesday	Wednesday	Thursday	Friday	Saturday
			1	2	3	4
5	6	7	8	9	10	11
12	13	14	15	16	17	18
19	20	21	22	23	24	25
26	27	28	29	30	31	

breezy

calm

windy

Help children find and name the day's date. Check your wind flag. Add the appropriate symbol to the calendar.

Daily Message

Modeled Writing Model the return sweep as you write the message. For example, as you come to the end of a line, you might say: *I am going to begin a new line of writing. Who can show me where to write the next word?*

Today is Thursday. We will read about animals that live on a farm.

Play "I Spy." *I spy a word with four letters. It begins with /s/ and ends with /d/. What is my word?* (*said*) Continue with other words. Let children make up their own clues when they understand the pattern.

Routines

Daily Phonemic Awareness
Blending Phonemes

- Read "Mix a Pancake" on page 35, and have children identify the word that ends in /ks/.

- Play a guessing game. *Let's put some sounds together to make words from the poem: /m//i//x/. Now you put the sounds for /m//i//x/ together. What do you get?* (mix)

- Continue the game by having children blend the sounds /i//t/ *it,* /p//o//p/ *pop,* /i//f/ *if,* and /c//a//n/ *can.*

- Have children use the words they made in oral sentences.

Higglety Pigglety: A Book of Rhymes, page 35

Getting Ready to Learn

To help plan their day, tell children that they will

- read the Science Link: *Who Lives on the Farm?*

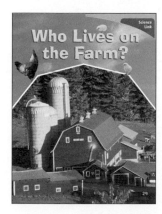

- make and read new words in the Phonics Center.

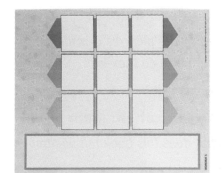

- reread "The Big, Big Box."

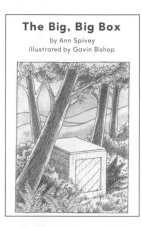

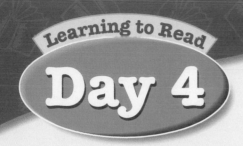

Big Book

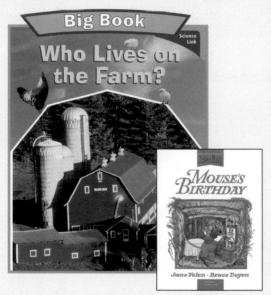

Who Lives on the Farm?

Science Link

Mouse's Birthday

Jane Yolen · Bruce Degen

pages 29–35

Oral Language

farm *We've read stories that take place on farms. Tell us what you know about who might live on a farm.*

 English Language Learners

Distribute pictures of animals and their homes, one to a child. Name the animals and their homes together. Then have children match the animals to their homes (duck-pond; horse-barn; and so on). Pairs can create sentences such as: *The duck lives in the pond.*

Sharing the Big Book
Science Link

▶ Building Background

Ask children to think about books about farms they have read. ***What animals live on farms? What people live on a farm?*** Read the title *Who Lives on the Farm?* and discuss a few pictures. Ask children to predict what animals will be in the book.

Reading for Understanding Pause for discussion as you share the article.

page 30

Strategy: Question

Student Modeling Remind children that it helps to ask questions as we read and then to look and listen for answers. Read the first few pages, pausing as you read. ***What questions do you have about this article? Do the words or pictures answer your questions?*** Read on, and have children tell if their questions were answered.

 Comprehension Focus: Noting Important Details

Student Modeling *What do you notice on this page? What does this tell you about who lives on a farm?*

pages 30–35

Compare and Contrast

- *Look at the pictures carefully. Do all the animals on the farm live in the barn? Where else do they live?* (No, they live in the meadow, a pond, a house, a hive.)

pages 30–35

Text Organization: Main Idea

- *What does this book tell us about?* (the animals and people who live on a farm)

Who lives in the meadow?
Baa, baa! The sheep.

Who lives in the hive?
Buzz, buzz! The bees.

30

31

pages 30–31

Who lives in the sty?
Oink, oink! The pigs!

Who lives in the pond?
Quack, quack! The ducks!

32

33

pages 32–33

Who lives on the farm?
Hello! The farmer!

Have you been to a farm?
Who lives there?

34

35

pages 34–35

pages 34–35

Concepts of Print

✓ **Directionality: Left to Right**

■ Point to the left side of the page. Tell children that this is where you start to read. Have them watch as you read, tracking the print with your finger or a pointer.

▶ Responding

Retelling Ask children which animals they would like to see in real life. Have volunteers summarize the information in the article, using the photographs as prompts.

Challenge

Ask children who are ready for a challenge to browse through the book with partners, looking for words they can read.

DAY 4

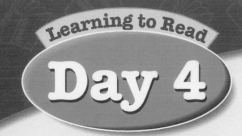

Teacher's Note

Children may sometimes ask how to spell words from the *-ox* family. Help them find *box* on the Word Wall and substitute the appropriate initial consonant.

Phonics

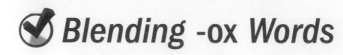

✓ Blending -ox Words

▶ Connect Sounds to Letters

Review Consonant *x* Using self-stick notes, cover the words on page 25 of *From Apples to Zebras.* Then display the page. As children name each picture, have them listen for the sound of the letter *x* in its final position. Uncover the words so that children can see the letters in the words.

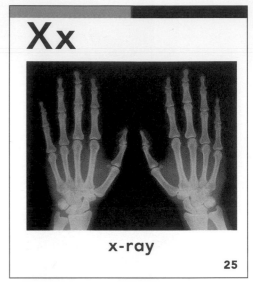

Xx

x-ray

25

From Apples to Zebras: A Book of ABC's, page 25

Reviewing -*ox* Remind children that to write words with *x* they also need a vowel ("helper letter") because every word has at least one of those. Ask which Alphafriend stands for the vowel sound /ŏ/. (Ozzie Octopus) Display Ozzie and help children name more words that start with /ŏ/. (*October, on, otter,* and *opposite*)

Hold up Letter Cards *b, o* and *x*. *Watch and listen as I write a Word Wall word: /b/ /ŏ/ /ks/,* box, */b/ /ŏ/ /ks/,* box.

Blending -*ox* Words Put the Letter Card *f* in front of *ox*. *Now let's read my new word: /f/ /oks/,* fox. Continue, having volunteers build and read *lox*. Some children might suggest nonsense words.

▶ Apply

Make word cards for *big* and *box*. Choose a child to spell *box* as you make the card. Build a sentence in a pocket chart, using the cards shown. Children read as you point.

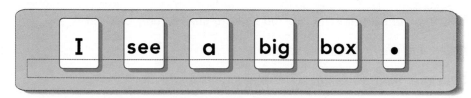

Repeat the activity with *Here is a big box* and *The fox ran to the* (Picture Card: *hen*). Choose a child to read the sentences as you give support.

Practice Book page 241 Children will complete this page at small group time.

Phonics Library In groups today, children will read *-ox* words as they reread the **Phonics Library** story "The Big, Big Box." See suggestions, page T89.

Practice Book p. 241

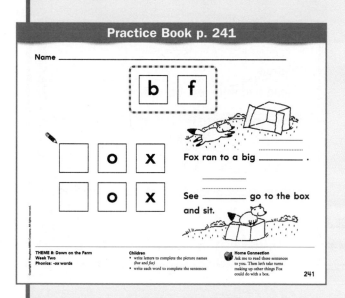

At Group Time

Phonics Center

Use the Phonics Center materials for **Theme 8, Week 2, Day 4**.

Diagnostic Check

If...	You can...
children do not easily participate in word-building activities,	make it more fun by building words using cereal or macaroni letters.

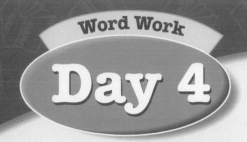

Day 4

► Word Families: *-ox, -ot, -ig*

Model how to build *ox* in a pocket chart, saying the word slowly to hear the sounds. *Who remembers how to spell* box? *Which letter do you hear first?*

Next, follow the Word Change routine. Children write the answers to your prompts.

- *Write* box. *You can find the letters in the pocket chart.*

- *Now think of how to write* lox. *You need to change only one letter.*

- *Listen:* lot. *Change two letters this time.*

- *Write* pot. *Think about the letter that stands for */p/.*

- *Now write* pig. *Listen */p / / ig /,* pig.

OBJECTIVES

Children

- read and write *-ox, -ot, -ig* words

MATERIALS

- **Letter Cards** *b, d, f, g, i, l, o, p, t, x*

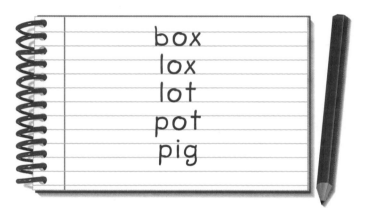

Interactive Writing

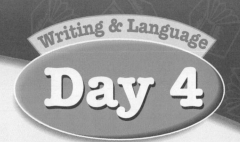

▶ Using Naming Words

Speaking and Writing Look back at the note children wrote for Mouse. (See page T91.) Help them notice its form, commenting specifically on the greeting and the closing. Call out some naming words that the group suggested.

■ Tell children that they can write a thank-you note, too. Choose someone you think deserves or would appreciate a note of thanks and model writing conventions as you write.

■ *Let's think about why we are writing this note. We want to thank (name) for something, so we'll say that first.*

■ *Who remembers how the note should start? Help me.*

■ Classroom—*that's a good naming word.*

■ *Look! I wrote* Mr. *in the first line. The second time I write it, it looks just the same.*

■ *What mark shall I write after the question?*

■ *Let's decide how to sign our note.*

Dear Mr. Bushy,

Thank you for cleaning our classroom every day. Do you like Mr. Bunny? We do.

Your friends,

Mrs. Tippet's Class

DAY 4

Day at a Glance

Learning to Read

Revisiting the Literature:

The Enormous Turnip, Mouse's Birthday, Who Lives on the Farm?, "The Big, Big Box"

✓ **Phonics: Review Consonant *x*; *-ox* Words; *page T104***

Word Work

Building Words, *page T106*

Writing & Language

Independent Writing, *page T107*

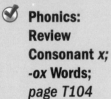 **Half-Day Kindergarten**

✓ Indicates lessons for tested skills. Choose additional activities as time allows.

Opening

Calendar

Sunday	Monday	Tuesday	Wednesday	Thursday	Friday	Saturday
			1	2	3	4
5	6	7	8	9	10	11
12	13	14	15	16	17	18
19	20	21	22	23	24	25
26	27	28	29	30	31	

calm

breezy

windy

Help children find and name the day and date. As you talk about the weather encourage children to use describing words.

Daily Message

Interactive Writing Share the pen: In the daily message, occasionally ask a child to contribute words or letters they can read and write.

We read about farm animals this week.
Danielle has seen a cow.
Paul has seen a goat.

Read the Word Wall together. Then play a guessing game: Read the wall again, after saying, *I'm thinking of a word on the wall; the word is see. Find it with your eyes. I'll point to some words. When I point to see, clap.* Continue the game, using other words from the Word Wall.

✔ Daily Phonemic Awareness
Blending Phonemes

- Read "Notice" in *Higglety Pigglety: A Book of Rhymes*, page 20.

- Play a guessing game. **Let's put some sounds together to make words from the poem:** / d / / o / / g / (dog); / c / / a / / t / (cat); / g / / o / / t / (got); / h / / a / / t / (hat). Continue with *pig, lit, sat, fit, fog, hog.*

Higglety Pigglety: A Book of Rhymes, page 20

Getting Ready to Learn

To help plan their day, tell children that they will

- reread and talk about books they've read this week.

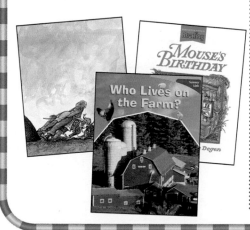

- take home a story they can read.

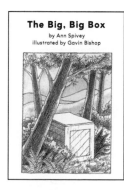

- write stories in their journals.

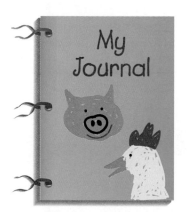

DAY 5

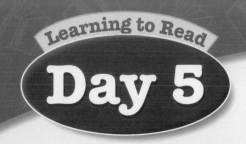

Revisiting the Literature

....

▶ Literature Discussion

Today children will compare the books you shared this week: *Mouse's Birthday, The Enormous Turnip, Who Lives on the Farm?,* and "The Big, Big Box." First, use these suggestions to help children recall the selections:

■ Have volunteers page through *Mouse's Birthday* and describe their favorite episode. Ask children to explain why Mouse's new home might be even better than his old one.

■ Reread page 35 from the article *Who Lives on the Farm?* and have a child name the animals shown.

■ Recall the story *The Enormous Turnip.* Ask why the mouse thought he got the job done.

■ Ask children what all these books have in common. (They are all about farm animals, farms, farmers.)

■ Have children reread "The Big, Big Box." Choose children to point to and read selected *-ot* and *-ox* words.

■ Ask children to vote for their favorite book of the week. Then read aloud the text of the winner.

 ## Comprehension: Noting Important Details

Comparing Books Tell children that each book they read this week has important details in the words and the pictures. Browse through each selection, inviting comments about what the book is about and what children liked about each story.

www.eduplace.com
Log on to **Education Place** for more activities relating to Down on the Farm.

www.bookadventure.org
This Internet reading-incentive program provides thousands of titles for children to read.

Building Fluency

▶ Rereading Familiar Texts

Phonics Library: "The Big, Big Box" Remind children that they've learned the new word *the* this week, and that they've learned to read words with *-ox*. As children reread "The Big, Big Box," have them look for words with *-ox*.

Review Feature several familiar **Phonics Library** titles in the Book Center. Have children demonstrate their growing reading skills by choosing one to reread to a friend or to a child from another class. Children can also choose to read it independently in the Book Center. From time to time, choose specific children to point out words or phrases.

Oral Reading Frequent rereadings of familiar texts help children develop confidence in their reading ability. As they gain confidence, they choose to read more often. Have children demonstrate their skills in small groups, explaining their own strategies for figuring out words, for rereading for sense, and for deriving meaning from text.

Dot Got a Big Pot
by Ann Spivey
illustrated by Ashley Wolff

The Big, Big Box
by Ann Spivey
illustrated by Gavin Bishop

A Pot For Dan Cat
by Ann Spivey
illustrated by Gavin Bishop

Blackline Master 36 Children complete the page and take it home to share their reading progress.

My Reading Log

I can read

My new words

said   the

Leveled Books

The materials listed below provide reading practice for children at different levels.

Little Big Books

Little Readers for Guided Reading

Houghton Mifflin Classroom Bookshelf

DAY 5

Home Connection

Remind children to share the take-home version of "The Big, Big Box" with their families.

Day 5

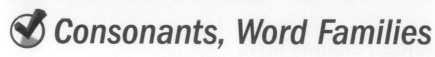

Phonics Review
✓ Consonants, Word Families

▶ Review

Tell children that they'll be word builders and word readers. Word builders stand with you at the chalkboard.

- ■ *Let's build* ox. *Listen:* /ŏ/ /ks/. *Write the letters.*

- ■ Children copy *ox* on the board and read the word.

- ■ Add *b*. Children ask the word readers what word they've written.

- ■ A new group changes places with the first one. At your directions, they erase the *b*, write *f*, and ask the word readers to say the new word.

- ■ Continue until everyone builds a word by replacing one letter. Examples: *fig, box, pot, fox, lot, pig, got, lox, hot, dig, pox, big.*

High-Frequency Word Review

✓ I, see, my, like, a, to, and, go, is, here, for, have, said

▶ Review

Display Word Cards for the words children have learned. Celebrate all the words children can recognize and read. Give a sentence starter of one or two words. Then choose children to make sentences. Have all children write and read aloud one sentence from the Word Cards you've displayed.

▶ Apply

Practice Book page 242 Children can complete this page independently and read it to you during small group time.

Phonics Library Have children take turns reading aloud to the class. Each child might read one page of "The Big, Big Box," "Dot Got a Big Pot," or a favorite **Phonics Library** selection from the previous theme. Remind readers to share the pictures!

Questions for discussion:

■ *Find a word in "The Big, Big Box" that ends with the same sound you hear at the beginning of Mr. X-Ray's name:/ks/. Point to the word and read it.*

■ *This week we added the word* the *to the Word Wall. Find the word* the *in "The Big, Big Box."*

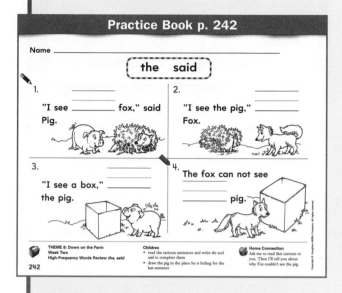

Practice Book p. 242

Portfolio Opportunity
Save selected Practice Book pages to demonstrate children's growing bank of high-frequency words.

Diagnostic Check

If . . .	You can . . .
children need help remembering a consonant's sound,	have them listen to the Alphafriend Audiotape in the Listening Center.
children pause at high-frequency words in **Phonics Library** selections,	have them read the book with a partner.

DAY 5

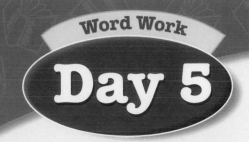

Word Work

Day 5

OBJECTIVES

Children

• build and read *-ox*, *-ot*, and *-ig* words.

MATERIALS

• **Letter Cards** *t, d, f, g, w, i, l, o, p, x*

Building Words

▶ Word Families: *-ox, -ot, -ig*

Follow the Word Change routine. Choose a child to build and read *ox*. Along the bottom of a pocket chart, line up the letters *b* and *f*. *Now listen: fffox. You say it. Who can tell us the letter I need to make* fox?

■ *Listen carefully, I'll give you a word. You write it.*

■ *Change* fox *to* pox.

■ *Change* pox *to* pot.

■ *Change* pot *to* lot.

■ *Change* lot *to* dot.

■ *Change* dot *to* dig.

■ *Change* dig *to* wig.

■ *Change* wig *to* fig.

■ *Change* fig *to* fox.

■ *Now we're back where we started.*

Note that some children will be able to do all these tasks; others, only a few.

Independent Writing

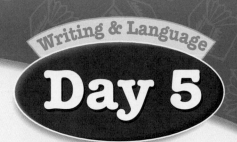
▶ Journals

As children write in their journals, have them write or draw about something they learned about farm animals. Remind them that good writers use naming words and action words to make their writing more interesting. Encourage writers to label their pictures, saying the words slowly and writing the letters they hear. Tell children to spell Word Wall words correctly, checking as they write.

Choose children who wish to take the author's chair and let them share their work with others.

OBJECTIVES

Children
- write independently

MATERIALS
- journals

Teacher's Note

Some children may need more prompts to write a story. Encourage these children to act out a story about the mouse house they created, and then ask them to write about it.

DAY 5

English Language Learners

MEETING INDIVIDUAL NEEDS

English language learners will be at different confidence levels with their writing abilities. They may feel more willing to try if they can write with a partner.

Literature for Week 3

Different texts for different purposes

Teacher Read Alouds:
- **The Story of Half-Chicken**
- **The Enormous Turnip**
- **A Lion on the Path**

Purposes

- oral language
- listening strategy
- comprehension skill

Big Books

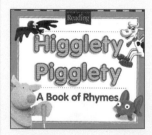

Higglety Pigglety: A Book of Rhymes

Purposes

- oral language development
- phonemic awareness

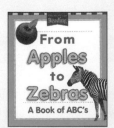

From Apples to Zebras: A Book of ABC's

Purposes

- alphabet recognition
- letters and sounds

Big Book: Main Selections

Purposes

- concepts of print
- reading strategy
- story language
- comprehension skills

Also available in Little Big Book and audiotape

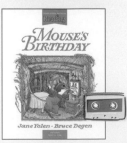

Also available in Little Big Book and audiotape

Leveled Books

Also in the Big Book:
- Social Studies Link
- Science Link

Purposes:
- reading strategies
- comprehension skills
- concepts of print

Phonics Library

Also available in Take-Home version

Purposes:
- applying phonics skills and high-frequency words

On My Way Practice Reader

To Fan Fox
by **Anne Myers**
page T153

Little Readers for Guided Reading
Collection K

Houghton Mifflin Classroom Bookshelf
Level K

www.eduplace.com
Log on to *Education Place* for more activities relating to *Down on the Farm.*

www.bookadventure.org
This free Internet reading incentive program provides thousands of titles for students to read.

Instructional Goals

Learning to Read

- ✓ *Phonemic Awareness:* Blending Phonemes

Strategy Focus: Evaluate, Monitor/Clarify

- ✓ *Comprehension Skill:* Inferences: Drawing Conclusions

- ✓ *Phonics Skills*

Phonemic Awareness: Beginning Sounds /h/, /f/, and /s/

Initial Consonants *H, h, F, f,* and *S, s;* Short *o + t*

Compare and Review: Initial Consonants: *h, v, c*

- ✓ *High-Frequency Review Words:* the, said

- ✓ *Concepts of Print:* Recognizing the Use of All Capital Letters; Directionality and Return Sweep

Word Work

High-Frequency Word Practice: Word Families: *-ox, -ot,*

Writing & Language

Vocabulary Skill: Using Singular and Plural Naming Words

Writing Skill: Writing a Class Newsletter

✓ = tested skills

Leveled Books

Have children read in appropriate levels daily.

Phonics Library
On My Way Practice Readers
Little Big Books
Houghton Mifflin Classroom Bookshelf

Day 1

Opening Routines, *T114–T115*

Word | Wall

- **Phonemic Awareness:** Blending Phonemes

Teacher Read Aloud
A Lion on the Path, T116–T119
- **Strategy:** Evaluate
- **Comprehension:** Inferences: Drawing Conclusions

Phonics

Instruction
- Phonemic Awareness, Beginning Sounds /f/, /h/, /s/, *T120–T121; Practice Book,* 245–246

High-Frequency Word Practice
- Words: *I, a, the, said, is, see, it, for, my, T122*

Oral Language
- Using Singular and Plural Naming Words, *T123*

Managing Small Groups
Teacher-Led Group
- Reread familiar **Phonics Library** selections

Independent Groups
- Finish *Practice Book, 243–246*
- *Phonics Center:* Theme 8, Week 3, Day 1
- Book, Art, other Centers

Day 2

Opening Routines, *T124–T125*

Word | Wall

- **Phonemic Awareness:** Blending Phonemes

Sharing the Big Book
Cows in the Kitchen, T126–T127
- **Strategy:** Evaluate
- **Comprehension:** Inferences: Drawing Conclusions

Phonics

Instruction, Practice
- Initial Consonant *f, h, s, T128–T129*
- *Practice Book,* 247

High-Frequency Word
- Review Words: *the, said, T130–T131*
- *Practice Book,* 248

High-Frequency Word Practice
- Building Sentences, *T132*

Vocabulary Expansion
- Using Naming Words, *T133*

Managing Small Groups
Teacher-Led Group
- Begin *Practice Book, 247–248* and **Blackline Masters** 164 or 190, 178 or 204, and 159 or 185.

Independent Groups
- Finish *Practice Book, 247–248* and **Blackline Masters** 164 or 190, 178 or 204, and 159 or 185.
- *Phonics Center:* Theme 8, Week 3, Day 2
- Science, other Centers

Technology

Lesson Planner CD-ROM: Customize your planning for *Down on the Farm* with the Lesson Planner.

Day 3

Opening Routines, *T134–T135*

Word Wall

• **Phonemic Awareness:** Blending Phonemes

Sharing the Big Book
Mouse's Birthday, T136–T137
• **Strategy:** Evaluate
• **Comprehension:** Inferences: Drawing Conclusions, *T136; Practice Book, 249*
• **Concepts of Print:** Recognizing the Use of All Capital Letters, *T137*

Phonics

Practice, Application
• Review Consonant *h, T138–T139*

Instruction
• Blending *h -ot, T138–T139; Practice Book, 250*
• **Phonics Library:** "A Pot for Dan Cat," *T139*

Building Words
• Word Families: *-ot, -ox, T140*

✎ **Shared Writing**
• Writing a Class Newsletter, *T141*
• Viewing and Writing, *T141*

Managing Small Groups
Teacher-Led Group
• Read **Phonics Library** "A Pot for Dan Cat"
• Write letters *O, o;* begin **Blackline Masters 171** or **197**.
• Begin *Practice Book, 249–250*

Independent Groups
• Finish **Blackline Masters 171** or **197** and *Practice Book, 249–250.*
• Writing, Art, other Centers

Day 4

Opening Routines, *T142–T143*

Word Wall

• **Phonemic Awareness:** Blending Phonemes

Sharing the Big Book
Social Studies Link: "Ice Cream: From Cows to Kids!," *T144*
Science Link: "Who Lives on the Farm?," *T145*
• **Strategy:** Monitor/Clarify, Evaluate
• **Comprehension:** Inferences: Drawing Conclusions
• **Concepts of Print:** Directionality and Return Sweep

Phonics

Practice
• Blending *-ox* and *-ot* Words, *T146–T147; Practice Book, 251*

Building Words
• Word Families: *-ox, -ot, -ig, it, T148*

✎ **Interactive Writing**
• Speaking and Writing, *T149*
• Writing a Class Newsletter, *T149*

Managing Small Groups
Teacher-Led Group
• Reread **Phonics Library** selection "A Pot for Dan Cat"
• Begin *Practice Book, 251*

Independent Groups
• Finish *Practice Book, 251*
• *Phonics Center:* Theme 8, Week 3, Day 4
• Science, other Centers

Day 5

Opening Routines, *T150–T151*

Word Wall

• **Phonemic Awareness:** Blending Phonemes

Revisiting the Literature
Comprehension: Making Inferences, *T152*
Building Fluency
• On My Way Practice Reader: "To Fan Fox," *T153*

Phonics

Review
• Familiar Consonants; *-ox, -ot, -ig, T154*

High-Frequency Word Review
• Words: *I, see, my, like, a, to, and, go, is, here, for, have, said, T155; Practice Book, 242*

Building Words
• Word Families: *-ig, -ot, -ox, T156*

✎ **Independent Writing**
• Journals: Independent Writing, *T157*

Managing Small Groups
Teacher-Led Group
• Reread familiar **Phonics Library** selections
• Begin *Practice Book, 252,* **Blackline Master 36.**

Independent Groups
• Reread **Phonics Library** selections
• Finish P*ractice Book, 252,* **Blackline Master 36.**
• Centers

Setting up the Centers

Teacher's Note

Management Tip As the end of the year nears, children often need something new and exciting in Center activities. Try adding a new Center: Bookmaking, Printing, Music are a few ideas. Change the location and look of Centers. Replace a round table with a square one; add interesting artwork to the walls; restock the Writing Center with a new collection of fancy pens or markers, find colorful and elaborate stickers; or provide new journals or journal covers. In the Music Center, provide one or more tape recorders and classical music cassettes. Children can draw to the mood of the music.

Phonics Center

Materials • Phonics Center materials for Theme 8, Week 3

Children review *h*, *v*, *c* and their sounds this week. They make words with known consonants and the word families *-ot, -ox*. Prepare materials for the Day 1, 2 and 4 activities. Cut apart the letter grids and bag them in plastic by color. Put out the Workmats and the open the Direction Chart to the appropriate day. Follow the Phonics Center Routine. See pages T121, T129, and T147 for this week's Phonics Center activities.

Book Center

Materials • books about farms and farm animals

Look for books about farms and farm machinery. Some children are particularly interested in how things work. "How-to" articles are important additions to the Book Center, even if children cannot read them. They can learn a lot from looking at the photographs.

Writing Center

(**Materials** • crayons • markers • lined and unlined writing paper)

Children draw and label pictures about a birthday party they would like to have. See page T137 for this week's Writing Center activity.

Art Center

(**Materials** • shoeboxes • rubber bands)

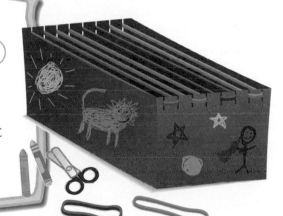

Children make a musical instrument to follow the Read Aloud story, *The Lion on the Path.* Emphasize the cross-curricular tie by talking about musical instruments from many cultures. Then have a concert with rhythm instruments and the model *mbiras* that children make in the Art Center. See page T117 for this week's Art Center activity.

Science Center

(**Materials** • drawing paper • crayons or markers • grocery circulars)

Children add to a feature analysis chant as they tell about animals. Later this week they talk about farms and farm produce, identifying, sorting, and classifying pictures of vegetables and grains. They also draw and label pictures of baby animals.

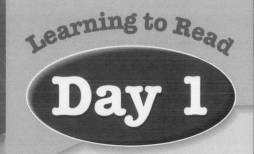

Day 1

Opening

Day at a Glance

Learning to Read

Teacher Read Aloud:

A Lion on the Path

☑ Reviewing *f, h, s,* page T120

Word Work

☑ **High-Frequency Word Practice,** page T122

Writing & Language

Oral Language, *page T123*

  Half-Day Kindergarten

☑ Indicates lessons for tested skills. Choose additional activities as time allows.

Calendar

Sunday	Monday	Tuesday	Wednesday	Thursday	Friday	Saturday
			1	2	3	4
5	6	7	8	9	10	11
12	13	14	15	16	17	18
19	20	21	22	23	24	25
26	27	28	29	30	31	

Point out and read the day and date. Ask children to notice and point out the use of capital letters on the calendar for the name of the month and for the days of the week.

Daily Message

Interactive Writing Share the pen; ask children to help write the beginning consonants of some of the words in the message. Notice and talk about why some will be in capitals.

> Today is Monday. We will read a story about a lion.

Have children chant the spelling of each word on the wall today: **t-h-e** *spells* the *and* s-a-i-d *spells* said *and* t-o *spells* to.

Routines

Daily Phonemic Awareness
Blending Phonemes

- Read "Mix a Pancake" on page 35 of *Higglety Pigglety*.

- After reading the poem, play a guessing game.

- *I'll say some sounds. You put them together to make words from the poem:* / m /... / i /... / x / (mix); / p /... / o /... / p / (pop); / c /... / a /... / n / (can).

- Continue for children who need more practice: *Sam, rap, fit, pan, lip, lot, hot, fox, sip.*

Mix a Pancake

Mix a pancake,
Stir a pancake,
Pop it in the pan;
Fry the pancake,
Toss the pancake —
Catch it if you can.

by Christina Rossetti

35

***Higglety Pigglety: A Book of Rhymes*, page 35**

Getting Ready to Learn

To help plan their day, tell children that they will

- listen to a story called *A Lion on the Path*.

- revisit some familiar Alphafriends: Hattie Horse, Fifi Fish, and Sammy Seal.

- make a musical instrument in the Art Center.

Day 1

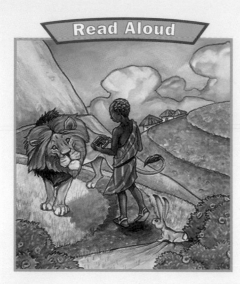

Read Aloud

Purposes • oral language • listening strategy • comprehension skill

Selection Summary
In this retelling of an old tale, a farmer, with the aid of a rabbit, uses music as a distraction to escape from a fierce lion.

Key Concepts
The shortest path is not always the best. Music has the power to soothe.

English Language Learners

Point to the mbira in the illustration, and invite children to talk about musical instruments they know. Mention that music calms the lion. Ask: *Does the same thing happen to people?* After reading, create a picture summary with input from children.

Teacher Read Aloud
Oral Language/Comprehension

▶ Building Background

Tell children that they are going to hear a story called *A Lion on the Path.* Guide a discussion about lions. Encourage the use of rich describing words: *fierce, tame, wild, frightening, stalk.*

Strategy: Evaluate

Teacher Modeling Model the Evaluate Strategy as you read. Tell children that readers often ask themselves how they feel about a story when they've finished. Remind children to listen for you to do that.

✓ Comprehension Focus: Inferences: Drawing Conclusions

Teacher Modeling Tell children that good readers often use what they know to figure out what happens in a story.

Think Aloud

This story is about a fierce lion. I've never met a lion. But I'll use what I know to help me understand how the people in the story feel.

▶ Listening to the Story

Read the story aloud using your voice to add drama and suspense to the tale. Pause to explain any unfamiliar vocabulary in this story. Note that the Read Aloud art is also shown on the back of the Theme Poster.

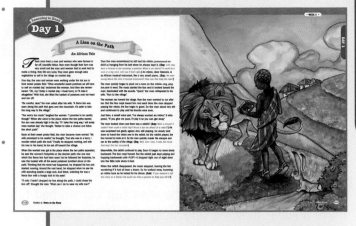

▶ Responding

Retelling the Story Help children summarize parts of the story.

- *Why didn't the woman go the long way to market?*

- *How did the woman feel when she met the lion? How do you know?*

- *What did the farmer do to help his wife escape from the lion?*

- *What happened at the end of the story? How did the rabbit help?*

Practice Book pages 243–244 Children will complete the pages during small group time.

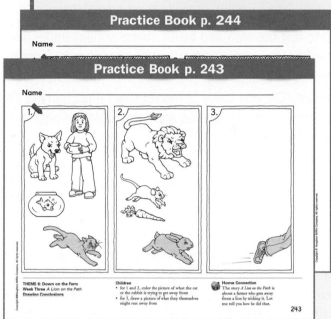

Practice Book p. 244

Practice Book p. 243

At Group Time

Art Center

(**Materials** • shoe boxes • rubber bands • scissors)

The farmer in the story played the *mbira* with his thumbs. Make a rubber band guitar by stretching sturdy rubber bands over slits cut in the ends of a shoebox. Children can "soothe the savage lion" by playing their own homemade mbiras.

Teacher's Note

Make a list of musical instruments children can name. As a challenge, have children name instruments that are "plucked."

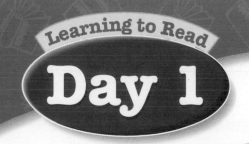

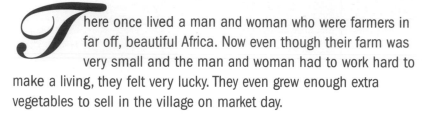

A Lion on the Path

An African Tale

There once lived a man and woman who were farmers in far off, beautiful Africa. Now even though their farm was very small and the man and woman had to work hard to make a living, they felt very lucky. They even grew enough extra vegetables to sell in the village on market day.

One day, the man and woman were working under the hot sun in their sweet potato field. "What wonderful sweet potatoes we will have to sell on market day," exclaimed the woman. And then she remembered. "Oh, my! Today *is* market day. I must hurry or I'll miss it altogether." With that, she lifted the basket of potatoes onto her head and ran off.

"Be careful, dear," the man called after his wife. "A fierce lion was seen along the path that goes over the mountain. It's safer to take the long way to the village."

"You worry too much," laughed the woman. "I promise to be careful, though." When she came to the place where the two paths started, the sun was already high in the sky. "If I take the long way, I will surely miss market day," she thought. "Better to take a chance and follow the short path."

Back at their sweet potato field, the man became more worried. "My wife promised to be careful," he thought, "but she was in a hurry. I wonder which path she took." Finally he stopped working, and with his hoe in his hand, he too set off toward the village.

When the worried man got to the place where the two paths separated, he saw the woman's footprints on the shorter path—the one near which the fierce lion had been seen! As he followed her footprints, he saw the basket with all the sweet potatoes tumbled about on the path. Thinking that the worst had happened, he dropped his hoe and started running. Around the next bend, he stopped when he saw his wife standing beside a large rock. And there, watching her was a fierce lion with a hungry look in his eyes!

"If only I hadn't dropped my hoe along the path, I could chase the lion off," thought the man. "What can I do to save my wife now?"

Then the man remembered he still had his mbira *(pronounced em-BEER-a)* hanging from his belt where he always kept it. **(Say:** *Let's stop here a minute to ask ourselves a question. What is an mbira? It could be a rock or a big stick. Let's see if that's right.***)** An mbira, dear listeners, is an African musical instrument, like a very small piano. **(Say:** *We were wrong about the rock. A musical instrument? How can this help the man?***)**

The man quickly began to pluck out a tune on the mbira—*ting, pling, link-plink* it went. The music startled the lion and it looked toward the man, fascinated with the sounds. "Quick," the man whispered to his wife. "Run to the village."

The woman ran toward the village. Now the man wanted to run after her. But the lion crept toward him. And each time the man stopped playing the mbira, the lion began to growl. So the man stood very still and continued to play until his thumbs were sore.

Just then, a small voice said, "I've always wanted an mbira." It whispered, "If you give me yours, I'll play it so you can get away."

The man looked down and there was a rabbit! **(Say:** *Wait a minute! A rabbit? How could a rabbit help? Would a lion be afraid of a rabbit?***)** He was surprised but gladly agreed. And, still playing, he slowly bent down to hand the mbira over to the rabbit. As the rabbit played, the lion turned to look at it. So the man quickly made his escape and ran to the safety of the village. **(Say,** *Well, now I see. It was the music that kept the lion occupied.***)**

Meanwhile, the rabbit continued to play. Soon it began to move slowly backward. The lion crept forward. But the rabbit just kept playing and hopping backwards until—PLOP!—it dropped right out of sight down into the little hole where it lived.

When the rabbit disappeared, the music stopped, leaving the lion wondering if it had all been a dream. So he walked away, humming an mbira tune as he looked for his dinner. **(Ask:** *If you wanted to tell this story to a friend, how would you draw a picture to help you tell it?***)**

Day 1

OBJECTIVES

Children

- identify pictures whose names begin with /h/, /f/, and /s/

MATERIALS

- **Alphafriend Cards** *Fifi Fish, Hattie Horse, Sammy Seal*
- **Alphafriend Audiotapes** Themes 2, 4, 5
- **Alphafolders** *Fifi Fish, Hattie Horse, Sammy Seal*
- **Picture Cards** for *f, h,* and *s,* and *black, lock, rock, pot, cat, jet*
- **Phonics Center:** Theme 8, Week 3, Day 1

Home Connection

Take-home versions of the songs for Fifi Fish, Hattie Horse, and Sammy Seal are on **Alphafriends Blackline Masters.** If children have not already taken these songs home to share with their families, you may want to have them do so now.

Phonemic Awareness
✓ Beginning Sounds

▶ Reviewing Alphafriends: Fifi Fish, Hattie Horse, and Sammy Seal

Remind children that they've met Fifi Fish, Hattie Horse, and Sammy Seal.

1 Alphafriend Riddles Read each clue.

- *Listen: This Alphafriend's sound is /f/. Say it with me: /f/.*

- *This animal is a fabulous swimmer. She has fins, not feet. Who is it?*

- Then help children recall /h/ for Hattie Horse and /s/ for Sammy Seal, using these clues:

- *This animal has hoofs instead of feet and hair called a mane.*

- *This Alphafriend likes to swim in the sea.*

2 Pocket Chart Display Fifi Fish, Hattie Horse, and Sammy Seal in a pocket chart. Say each name, emphasizing the initial sound slightly. Then have children try it.

3 📼 Alphafriend Audiotapes Play the three Alphafriends' songs.

4 Alphafolders Children can look at each illustration and name the /f/, /h/, and /s/ pictures.

5 Summarize

- *What are the names of these three Alphafriends? What are their sounds?*

- *What words in our Alphafriends' songs start with their sounds?*

- *Each time you see Fifi Fish remember /f/; for Hattie Horse, remember /h/; and for Sammy Seal, remember /s/.*

▶ Listening for /f/, /h/, and /s/

Compare and Review: /f/, /h/, /s/ Hold up the Picture Cards randomly, one at a time. Choose children to put the cards below the appropriate Alphafriends.

Pictures: *farm, feet, fork; horse, hen, hand; sad, salt, sandbox.*

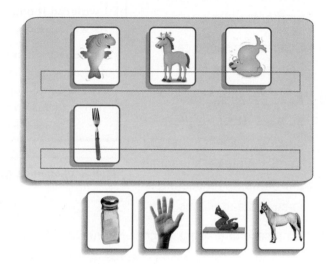

▶ Apply

Practice Book pages 245–246 Children will complete the pages at small group time.

At Group Time
Phonics Center

Use the Phonics Center materials for **Theme 8, Week 3, Day 1**.

Practice Book p. 246

Name _____

Practice Book p. 245

Name _____

1.

2.

3.

THEME 8: Down on the Farm
Week Three
Phonemic Awareness Review: /h/, /f/, /s/

Children
for each row,
• color the Alphafriend and two pictures whose names start like the Alphafriend's name (*Hattie Horse, Fifi Fish,* or *Sammy Seal*)
• draw another picture at the end of the row that starts with the same sound

Home Connection
Let me tell you about these Alphafriends and why I colored the pictures beside them. Then I'll tell you about the pictures I drew.

245

Day 1

High-Frequency Word Practice

OBJECTIVES

Children

- read high-frequency words
- create and write sentences with high-frequency words

MATERIALS

- **Word Cards** *a, for, I, is, it, my, said, see*
- ***Higglety Pigglety: A Book of Rhymes*** page 38
- **Punctuation Card:** period

Teacher's Note

If you have not already made word cards for the decodable words *cat, fox,* and *ox,* you will need to do so for this activity.

▶ Matching Words

- Distribute Word Cards for the high-frequency words *I, a, the, said, see, it, for,* and *my* to a group of children. Each child reads his or her word and finds its match on the Word Wall.

- Children exchange cards and read a new word.

- Read the poem "Tommy" on page 38 of *Higglety Pigglety.* Reinforce that the words children are learning are words they'll see often in stories and poems.

Tommy

I put a seed into the ground
And said, "I'll watch it grow."
I watered it and cared for it
As well as I could know.

One day I walked in my back yard,
And oh, what did I see!
My seed had popped itself right out,
Without consulting me.

by Gwendolyn Brooks

38

Higglety Pigglety: A Book of Rhymes, page 38

- On a second reading, track the print. Choose children to match words on their cards to the corresponding words in the poem.

Writing Opportunity Combine the Word Cards from above with *is, cat, ox,* and *fox* and build the sentences below. Children can then write and illustrate sentences of their own. Some will suggest their own ideas, too. Remind writers to use what they know about letters and sounds for words they choose.

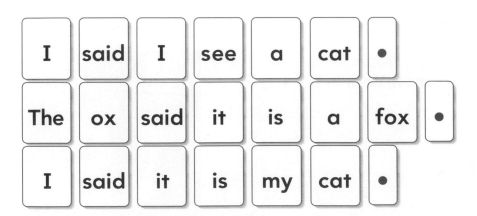

Oral Language

▶ Using Singular and Plural Naming Words

Browse through *Cows in the Kitchen* and *Mouse's Birthday.* Have children name the animals they see. Remind them that *cow, mouse, duck, pig, hen,* and *sheep* are naming words.

- ■ Now say: *Listen to these two words:* cow, cows. *What is the difference? Yes,* cows *means more than one. Here's another one:* pig, pigs. *Which word means more than one? It's your turn now:* duck (ducks)*;* hen (hens). *Say them with me. There's not much difference between the two words. But you must listen to the ending sound:* /s/.

- ■ Then tell children you'll teach them a tricky one. *What word means more than one mouse?* MICE! *It doesn't sound like* mouse. Make a chart like this.

Ask children what they notice. (An s is added to all but one word.)

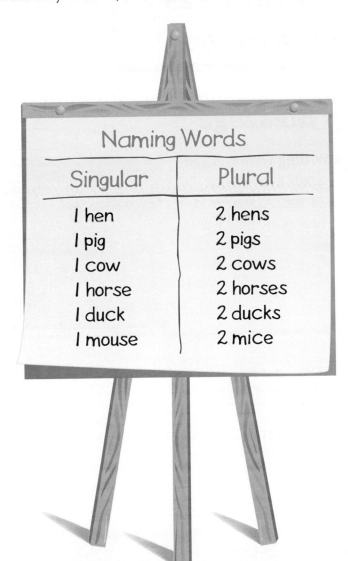

Naming Words

Singular	Plural
I hen	2 hens
I pig	2 pigs
I cow	2 cows
I horse	2 horses
I duck	2 ducks
I mouse	2 mice

OBJECTIVES

Children
- use singular and plural naming words

MATERIALS

- **Big Books:** *Cows in the Kitchen, Mouse's Birthday*

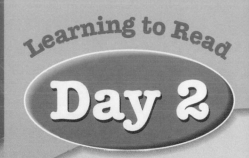

Day 2

Day at a Glance

Learning to Read

Big Book:

Cows in the Kitchen

☑ **Phonics: Initial Consonants h, f, s,** *page T128*

☑ **High-Frequency Words:** *the, said,* *page 130*

Word Work

High-Frequency Word Practice, *page T132*

Writing & Language

Vocabulary Expansion, *page T133*

 Half-Day Kindergarten

☑ Indicates lessons for tested skills. Choose additional activities as time allows.

Calendar

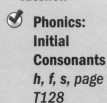

Sunday	Monday	Tuesday	Wednesday	Thursday	Friday	Saturday
			1	2	3	4
5	6	7	8	9	10	11
12	13	14	15	16	17	18
19	20	21	22	23	24	25
26	27	28	29	30	31	

Sun day
Mon day
Tues day
Wednes day
Thurs day
Fri day
Sat ur day

At calendar time, name each day of the week and clap the syllables. Discover the day that has more claps than the others.

Daily Message

Modeled Writing Have children read some words in the Daily Message with you. As they read, emphasize how many new words they've learned.

Mr. Burns said we can go to the farm on Monday. We can see some cows and some sheep. I like the pigs best.

Word Wall

Play "Pass the Pointer." Children can take turns finding Word Wall words with a pointer as you call them out.

Routines

 Daily Phonemic Awareness
Blending Phonemes

Play Four Square Words Follow the routine, having children fold papers in four. Use picturable words from recent word family lessons: *fox, pot, box,* and *cot.* Say a word slowly, one phoneme at a time. */f/... /o/... /x/. Say it with me: /f/... /o/... /x/. What word is it? Don't say it out loud. Draw a picture in one square. Remember the picture doesn't have to be fancy.... What picture did you draw?* When pictures have been identified, children show them to a partner and have the partner identify the word.

Getting Ready to Learn

To help plan their day, tell children that they will

- enjoy a favorite Big Book, *Cows in the Kitchen.*

- meet Fifi Fish, Hattie Horse, and Sammy Seal again.

- make a chart for the Science Center.

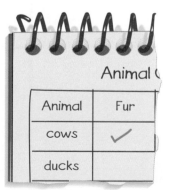

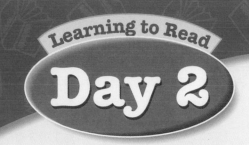

Big Book

Purposes • concepts of print • story language • reading strategy • comprehension skill

Extra Support

Take children on a picture walk to review the animals and their sounds. Preview a few of the rhyming couplets and have children chime in.

Sharing the Big Book
Oral Language/Comprehension

▶ Building Background

Reading for Understanding Browse through *Cows in the Kitchen* together. By now it may be an old favorite. Have children recall the mischief each animal got into in Farmer Tom's house. Emphasize the humor of the story, and enjoy the silliness of the illustrations and the rhyme.

Strategy: Evaluate

Teacher Modeling Remind children that the author, June Crebbin, wrote this story just for fun. Have children decide which incidents are the funniest. Which are the most ridiculous? Which made children laugh the most?

Think Aloud

I think this is one of my favorite books because it makes me laugh. This time when we read it, you decide which animal made you laugh the most. Then we'll talk about it later.

✓ Comprehension Focus: Inferences: Drawing Conclusions

Teacher Modeling Tell children that readers have to use what they already know to help them understand and enjoy a story. Using what you know helps you understand what has happened or what the author had in mind.

Think Aloud

I'll use what I know about farms and animals to figure out why this story is so funny. For example, I know that farmers don't just go to sleep and let their animals into the house. It helps me know that this is a silly story that June Crebbin, the author, wrote to make me laugh.

▶ Sharing the Story

Reread the story, emphasizing the clear and strong rhyming pattern. You could even sing parts of it to the tune of "Skip to My Lou." Pause briefly for discussion points.

pages 1–13

Make Inferences: Draw Conclusions

■ *If Tom Farmer were a real farmer, would he have let the animals in his farmhouse? How do you know? Who can find the pictures that show how tired Tom Farmer was? How do you know?* (He's lying in the haystack and he says, "Z-z-z-z-z.")

 pages 14–15

Concepts of Print: All Capital Letters

■ *Read these words after me ... . How can you tell that the author wants us to read with lots of expression?* (The words are printed in all capital letters.)

pages 2–25

Evaluate

■ *This story always makes me giggle. How do you feel about it?*

⸺⸺⸺⸺⸺⸺⸺⸺⸺⸺⸺⸺⸺⸺⸺⸺⸺⸺⸺⸺⸺⸺⸺⸺⸺⸺

▶ Responding

Dramatization Encourage children to work with partners to retell their favorite parts of the story. They can use the illustrations as prompts.

Science Center

Start a feature analysis chart, using the animals from *Cows in the Kitchen.* Talk about animal characteristics, and have children put a check mark next to each. Put the chart in the Science Center.

Animal Characteristics

Animal	Fur	Feathers	4 Legs	2 Legs
cows	✓		✓	
ducks		✓		✓
pigs	✓		✓	

 Challenge

Have children work with partners to "sing" the story text, using the illustrations and animal sounds they know.

 English Language Learners

Ask English language learners to retell the story. Next, have them work in small groups to think of other animals and places they could be in. For example: cows in the closet, hens at the hospital, goats in the garden, horses in the hall, and so on. Record their answers and have them illustrate to create a class book.

Extra Support

To help children who don't readily recognize the letters and sounds *h* /h/, *f* /f/ and *s* /s/, have them repeat a previous Phonics Center activity with you.

Phonics

✓ Initial Consonants f, h, s

▶ Develop Phonemic Awareness

Beginning Sounds Read this poem aloud, and have children echo it. Have them repeat /h/ words, hopping as they say each one. On a second recitation, children repeat /f/ words, moving arms like fins for swimming. The third time around, children repeat and snap (or) clap for /s/ words.

> While Hattie Horse is
> munching hay,
> Sammy Seal sails
> up to play.
> Then Fifi Fish floats
> by to say,
> "Let's have a fine and
> happy day!"

▶ Connect Sounds to Letters

Beginning Letters Display Hattie Horse, and name the letter *h*. Say, ***The letter* h *stands for* /h/*, as in* horse. *Your turn now. Write* h *in the air. What other words can the letter* h *stand for?* (hat, have, Hallie, happy) *Remember* Hattie Horse. *She'll help you remember what the letter looks like and what it sounds like,* /h/. Continue with Fifi Fish and Sammy Seal, using their names to remind children of the letter sounds. Sample answers might include *fan, fire, forest, Faith; sand, summer, suit, Sue.*

Compare and Review: *h, f, s*
In a pocket chart, display the Letter Cards. Place the Picture Cards in random order around the chart. Call on specific children to name a picture, say its beginning sound, and place it below the correct letter.

Tell children they will sort more pictures in the Phonics Center today.

▶ Handwriting

Writing *F, f; H, h; S, s* For children who need, practice, write the letters *F, f, H, h,* and *S, s.* Review how to write each letter, including where to begin each stroke. Some children will benefit from tracing the letters you've written.

Ff Hh Ss

▶ Apply

Practice Book page 247 Children will complete the page at small group time.

Blackline Masters 162, 164, 175 These provide additional handwriting practice.

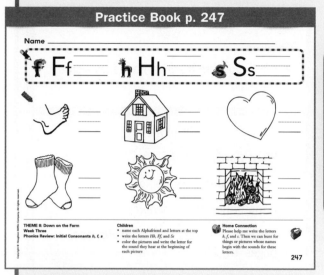

Practice Book p. 247

At Group Time

Phonics Center

Use the Phonics Center materials for **Theme 8, Week 3, Day 2.**

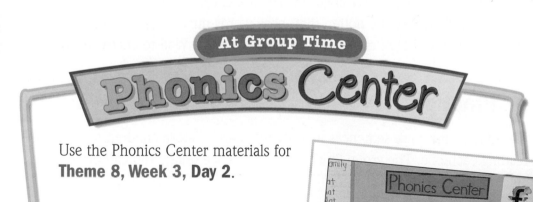

📎 Teacher's Note

Handwriting practice for the continuous stroke style is available on **Blackline Masters 188, 190, 201.**

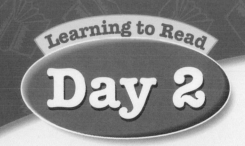

Learning to Read
Day 2

OBJECTIVES

Children

- read and write the high-frequency words the, said

MATERIALS

- **Word Cards** said, the, The
- **Picture Cards** cow, her, pig
- **Punctuation Card:** period
- **Higglety Pigglety: A Book of Rhymes,** pages 14, 27

✔ High-Frequency Words

Review Words: the, said

▶ Teach

Remind children they've learned two important new words recently: *the* and *said.* They are important because children read them often and use them every day when they speak. Tell children to listen for the word *the* in these sentences.

The rooster woke everyone on the farm. *The* farmer plowed the field. Then he planted *the* corn.

Choose a child to write *the*. If needed, remind the child to check the Word Wall for the correct spelling. **Write the on your white boards. Who will use it in a sentence of your own?**

Continue with *said*, using these context sentences:

The farmer *said* "Zzzz!"   The duck *said*, "Quack!"   The pig *said*, "Oink!"

Choose another child to write *said*. Children write the word and volunteers use it in sentences of their own.

Word Wall Have children clap and cheer for *the* and *said* on the Word Wall. Reinforce the notion that these words must be spelled correctly when writing. Children can always refer to the Word Wall to check the spelling.

▶ Practice

Reading Start these sentences in a pocket chart. Choose children to take turns reading each one. The group finishes each sentence orally. You can make speech balloons on index cards for the animal sounds. Children add end punctuation. In the Writing Center, children can draw and write additional sentences following the pattern. Remind them to use what they know about letters and sounds.

Display page 27 of *Higglety Pigglety.*

■ Emphasize the importance of knowing how to read *the* and *said*. Reinforce this by reading aloud "The Itsy Bitsy Spider." Have children listen for and find the word *the*. Ask what they notice about *The* in the title. (the capital letter)

■ Using the Word Card *the*, choose children to find and match it in the text. Then have the group recite the poem from memory and raise their hands each time they say *the*.

The Itsy Bitsy Spider

The itsy bitsy spider
Climbed up the waterspout.

Down came the rain
And washed the spider out.

Out came the sun
And dried up all the rain,

And the itsy bitsy spider
Climbed up the spout again.

27

Higglety Pigglety: A Book of Rhymes, **page 27**

■ Follow a similar procedure with "Little Arabella Stiller" on page 14. This time, look for the word *said*.

▶ Apply

Practice Book page 248 Children will read and write *the* and *said* as they complete the Practice Book page. On Day 3, they will practice reading high-frequency words in the **Phonics Library** story "A Pot for Dan Cat."

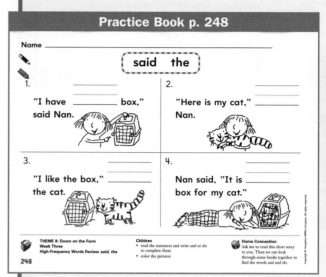

Practice Book p. 248

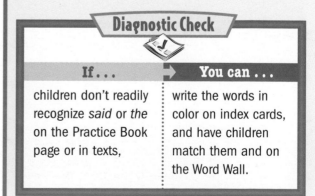

Diagnostic Check

If . . .	You can . . .
children don't readily recognize *said* or *the* on the Practice Book page or in texts,	write the words in color on index cards, and have children match them and on the Word Wall.

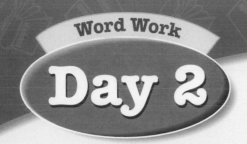

OBJECTIVES

Children

• read high-frequency words

• write sentences with high-frequency words

High-Frequency Word Practice

▶ Building Sentences

Remind children that when June Crebbin wrote *Cows in the Kitchen,* she used lots of animal sounds. Using index cards for speech balloon words, model how to write a sentence, highlighting words children can read and write.

■ *Suppose we wanted to write about animals as June Crebbin did. Here's a sentence we could start with. Listen:* The cat said M-e-o-w! *Who will spell the first word* The? *Think carefully. Does it have a capital? Why?*

■ *I'll leave a space after the word* The *so I can start the word cat.*

■ *Who'll write* cat *for us? Say it slowly and write the letters you hear. ... Now who will write* said?

■ *Remember what the cat says: M-e-o-w. What letter do you hear first? I must remember to put quotation marks around* Meow *because it's what the cat* said.

■ *Let's read together. Look how many words you can read and write!*

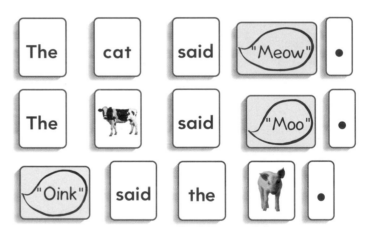

Writing Opportunity Post the animals' conversation in the Writing Center. Children can read it and add sentences of their own based on the pattern. Remind children that they can use temporary phonics spellings by saying words slowly and writing the letters they hear.

Vocabulary Expansion

▶ Using Naming Words

■ Expand children's vocabulary in this lesson about farm animals and their babies. Begin by talking about familiar animals' babies. *Puppies* and *kittens* are familiar words for most children. You might want to review the animals children read about in *Mouse's Birthday* and *Cows in the Kitchen.*

■ *Let's think about the animals in the Big Books we've read. Who knows what baby cows are called? Right, a baby cow is called a calf. Let's think about more babies.*

■ Assess children's oral vocabularies as you engage them in conversation. Make a chart like the one shown. Hang it in the Writing Center or in the Science Center. Illustrations help children use the chart more effectively.

Animal		Baby	
dog		puppy	
cat		kitten	
pig		piglet	
cow		calf	
goat		kid	

At Group Time
Science Center

Have children fold papers in half. They draw a baby animal on one side and the adult animal on the other. They can describe their drawings to a partner. Partners can label the drawings using the chart or another word, if they added their own idea.

Extra Support

For some children, farm animals may not be at all familiar. Read aloud an assortment of books about farms and farm animals and then place them in the Book Corner for browsing. Search your school library for books about baby animals, too.

English Language Learners

Show learners separate pictures of adult animals and their babies. Introduce new vocabulary such as *piglet, colt, lamb, duckling,* and so on. Put the cards on the floor, and ask children to pick up the two that are related, for example, *cow-calf.*

Day 3

Day at a Glance

Learning to Read

Big Book:

Mouse's Birthday

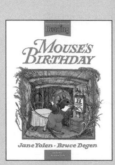

✓ **Phonics:** Blending *h -ot,* page T138

Word Work

Building Words, *page T140*

Writing & Language

Shared Writing, *page T141*

☀ Half-Day Kindergarten

✓ Indicates lessons for tested skills. Choose additional activities as time allows.

Opening

Calendar

Sunday	Monday	Tuesday	Wednesday	Thursday	Friday	Saturday
			1	2	3	4
5	6	7	8	9	10	11
12	13	14	15	16	17	18
19	20	21	22	23	24	25
26	27	28	29	30	31	

March May

Review the day and date. Talk about the name of the month. If it is possible, have children suggest another month that begins with the same sound.

Daily Message

Modeled Writing Tie your daily message to the theme. Then talk about print conventions. *Mr. Sutter's name begins with capital letters just like your names do. We always put a period after Mr. Did I leave enough space between my words?*

I drove by Mr. Sutter's farm today. The cows were sitting down. I wonder if cows like windy weather.

Play "I Spy" with the Word Wall words. *I spy a word that starts with /g/ and means the opposite of stop. Find it with your eyes. Then I'll ask someone to point to it.* Choose a child to read the word. Give similar clues for other words.

....

✓ Daily Phonemic Awareness
Blending Phonemes

- Read "Mix a Pancake" on page 35 in *Higglety Pigglety: A Book of Rhymes.*

- Play Mr. FunnyWord. Remind children that Mr. FunnyWord likes words from the poem. *Remember that Mr. FunnyWord says words in a funny way. Teach Mr. FunnyWord how to say the words. Listen: /m//i//x/. What's Mr. FunnyWord saying? Think it first. Then say it out loud. That's right! He's trying to say* mix.

- Continue with other poem words *pop, pan, can.* Add more words for children to blend: *sip, tap, lip, fox, box, tip, lap, sit.*

Mix a Pancake

Mix a pancake,
Stir a pancake,
Pop it in the pan;
Fry the pancake,
Toss the pancake —
Catch it if you can.

by Christina Rossetti

35

Higglety Pigglety: A Book of Rhymes, page 35

Getting Ready to Learn

To help plan their day, tell children that they will

- reread a favorite Big Book: *Mouse's Birthday.*

- read a story called "A Pot for Dan Cat."

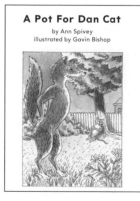

- draw and write about a birthday party.

My Birthday Party

DAY 3

Big Book

Reading

MOUSE'S BIRTHDAY

Jane Yolen · Bruce Degen

Includes
Science Link

Purposes • concepts of print • story language
• reading strategy • comprehension skill

Sharing the Big Book
Oral Language/Comprehension

▶ Building Background

Reading for Understanding Reintroduce *Mouse's Birthday*. Have children share what they remember about the story, recalling favorite scenes and happenings. Then read the story again, reminding children to listen for their favorite parts.

Strategy: Evaluate

Teacher-Student Modeling Remind children that some stories are written just for fun. Ask them to listen for and share the parts they think are funniest.

Think Aloud

I liked the part where the horse squeezed into Mouse's house on his knees. I thought that was funny. Tell the part you think is funniest.

✔ Comprehension Focus:
Inferences: Drawing Conclusions

Teacher-Student Modeling Remind children that using what they know helps them understand what will happen in a story.

Think Aloud

You know how small a mouse is. And you know how big a horse is. So a horse can't fit into a mouse's hole. So you're not surprised when the mouse's house bursts at the seams, are you? Let's remember that when we listen to the story.

Extra Support

Page through the book with a small group to review the characters who attend Mouse's party. Recall what each character brought, beginning with the repetitive phrase *In came (name) upon his knees, carrying a gift of (gift).*

▶ Sharing the Story

Reread the story, pausing for these discussion points:

 pages 1–5

Making Inferences: Drawing Conclusions

■ *What do we know about Mouse's house?* (It's very small.) *What do we know about Mouse's guests?* (They're very big.) *So what will probably happen?* (They'll burst the house.)

 page 16

Concepts of Print: Use of All Capital Letters

■ *Which words are written in capital letters? How do you think we should read them? Let's shout* Happy Birthday, Mouse! *while I point.*

pages 2–26

Evaluate

■ *Did you think this story was funny? What was your favorite part?*

▶ Responding

Retelling the Story Make a circle map to help children retell *Mouse's Birthday*. Encourage the use of sequence words.

Practice Book, page 249 Children complete the page at small group time.

At Group Time

Writing Center

Have children draw pictures of a birthday party they'd like to have. Have them draw people who might attend and gifts they might bring. Label pictures for children.

My Birthday Party

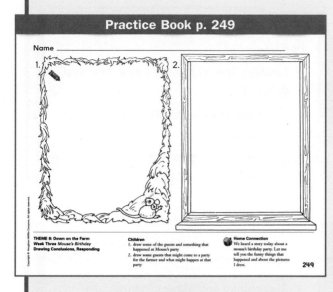
Practice Book p. 249

Mouse's Birthday

Teacher's Note

Stress creativity as children write about a birthday party. Assure them that they can write about a party they've had or one they'd like to have. The party can be as real or as fanciful as they'd like.

DAY 3

Practice Book p. 250

Name _____

| See | fox | hot |

1. See the fat _____ ? ☺ ☹

2. _____ the pig? ☺ ☹

3. See the _____ fox? ☺ ☹

THEME 8: Down on the Farm
Week Three
Phonics Review: *a, f, h, -ot, -ox*

Children
- read the questions and write *See, fox* and *hot* to complete them
- mark yes (smile) or no (frown) to show whether the pictures answer the questions

Home Connection
Let me read these questions to you. Then we can cut the sentences into separate words, scramble them, and build the sentences again.

250

Extra Support

Write *pot* on an index card, and *c, h, d, p, n,* and *g* on small, self-stick notes. Staple the "stickies" over the *p* in *pot*. Have children take turns flipping the stickies and reading the new words.

Phonics

✓ *Blending* h -ot

▶ Connect Sounds to Letters

Review Consonant *h* Play Hattie Horse's song, and have children say / h / and pat their heads for / h / words. Write *H* and *h* on the board, and sing the song again. Point to the letters for each / h / word.

Blending *-ot* Reintroduce Alphafriend Ozzie Octopus, and remind children that Ozzie's letter *o* is a vowel or a "helper letter". Remind children that *t* stands for the / t / sound. Model blending the *-ot* as you hold the Letter Cards apart and then together. *The sound for o is first, and the sound for t is last. Listen: / ŏ / / t /, ot.* Move the cards together. Choose a child to move cards as classmates blend. *I'll make the word* hot *with Letter Cards. Which sound do you hear first?... next?... last?*

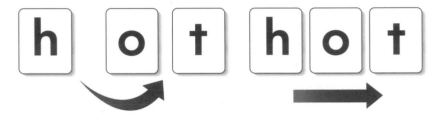

Blending *-ot* Words Have children replace *h* with *n* and read the word *not*. Continue having them build and read *cot, pot, dot,* and *got*.

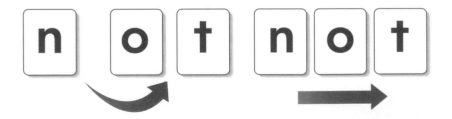

Word Wall Have children find and read the word *pot* on the Word Wall. Remind them to use the Word Wall to help them spell *pot* and other words in the *-ot* family.

▶ Apply

Practice Book page 250 Children complete the page at small group time.

Phonics
in Action

Applying Phonics Skills and High-Frequency Words

Purposes
- apply phonics skills
- read high-frequency words

A Pot For Dan Cat
by Ann Spivey
illustrated by Gavin Bishop

17

"I can see Dan Cat," said Fan Fox.

18

Fan Fox ran.
Dan Cat ran.

19

Phonics/Decoding Strategy

Teacher-Student Modeling Remind children of the steps in the Phonics/Decoding Strategy. When possible, have children model the strategy for the group.

Think Aloud

Here's what I do when I come to a word I don't know. First I look at the letters and think about their sounds. I blend the sounds together. Let's try it together with the title. I know the first word, A. It's a capital letter because it's in the title. The next word starts with p. P stands for /p/. I know the sounds for o and t, -ot. So the word is pot. Now let's read the whole title together.

Dan Cat can see a big, big pot.
Can Dan Cat fit?

20

Dan Cat can fit!
Fan Fox ran and ran.

21

During a picture walk, introduce Dan Cat and Fan Fox and set the scene for a story in which Cat cleverly outsmarts her friend Fox. *You read the title, "A Pot for Dan Cat." Now what do you think a cat will do with a pot? Does that make sense? Maybe it will after we read the story.*

Dan Cat sat.

22

▶ Coached Reading

Because most kindergartners are not yet reading silently, encourage them to "whisper read." Prompts:

page 18 *Fan Fox says that she can see Dan Cat. What do you think she'll do?*
(Play chase. Run after him.)

page 19 *Oh no! Fan Fox is chasing Dan Cat. Who can read the words? Knowing what you know about foxes and cats, who will win the chase? Let's read to find out.*

page 20 *What does Dan Cat see? Read what it says. Everyone point to the -ot word. Read it together.*

page 21 *Did Dan Cat fit? Read the words that tell the answer.*

page 22 *What happens at the end of the story? Let's read what the words say.*

Home Connection

Children can color the pictures in their take-home version of "A Pot for Dan Cat." After reading on Day 4, they can take it home to read to family members.

DAY 3

Building Words

▶ Word Families -*ot*, -*ox*

Using the Letter Cards, have children build the word *ox*. **Listen to the word. How many sounds do you hear? What letters stand for those sounds?**

Have everyone read *ox*. Then ask which letter they need to make *pox*. Choose a child to write *pox* and read it for others.

Now what happens if I change x to t? Who will read the word? Who will write not? fox? lox? got? Note: it is important to mix examples so that children are not merely substituting the initial consonants.

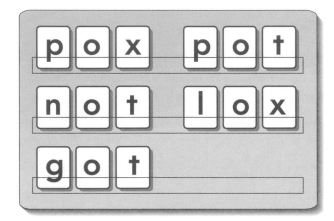

Small groups of children who need more practice can work together writing -*ox* and -*ot* words using stamps, a computer, magnetic letters, or other manipulatives in your collection. Some children may write nonsense words. Have them read the words aloud.

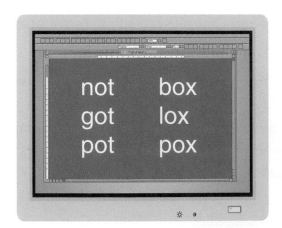

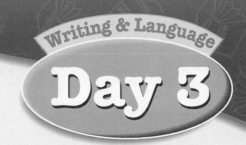
Shared Writing

▶ Writing a Class Newsletter

Viewing and Writing Bring in an appropriate page from a local newspaper. Have children look at it and discuss the pictures and the headlines. Help children understand how a newspaper tells readers what is happening in the community. Tell children they can write news of what *they've* done in school to share with their families.

■ Display the theme's Big Books. Recall center activities. Talk about important events. Then begin to write together. Model good writing habits as you share your news.

■ *Look, the newspaper I brought has a name,* **The Sentinel.** *What can we call our newsletter? I'll write it at the top.*

■ *The newspaper has the important news in the most important spot. What is most important in our classroom? We will write it at the top, too. What will we use as a headline? It should be attention-getting. Should we include a picture? We can draw it later. But we'll leave a space for it here. What else should we write about?*

OBJECTIVES

Children
• learn the purpose and form of a newspaper
• share the writing of a class newsletter

DAY 3

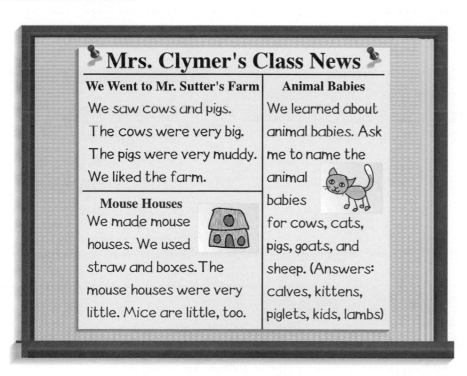

Mrs. Clymer's Class News

We Went to Mr. Sutter's Farm	**Animal Babies**
We saw cows and pigs. The cows were very big. The pigs were very muddy. We liked the farm.	We learned about animal babies. Ask me to name the animal babies
Mouse Houses We made mouse houses. We used straw and boxes. The mouse houses were very little. Mice are little, too.	for cows, cats, pigs, goats, and sheep. (Answers: calves, kittens, piglets, kids, lambs)

Day at a Glance

Learning to Read

Big Books:

Ice Cream: From Cows to Kids!/
Who Lives on the Farm?

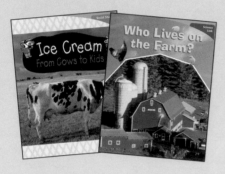

✓ **Phonics: Reviewing / f /, / h /,**
/ s /; Blending -ot and -ox Words,
page T146

Word Work

Building Words, *page T148*

Writing & Language

Interactive Writing, *page T149*

 Half-Day Kindergarten

✓ Indicates lessons for tested
skills. Choose additional
activities as time allows.

Opening

Calendar

Sunday	Monday	Tuesday	Wednesday	Thursday	Friday	Saturday
			1	2	3	4
5	6	7	8	9	10	11
12	13	14	15	16	17	18
19	20	21	22	23	24	25
26	27	28	29	30	31	

Name the days of the week,
chanting them in a lively
manner. Match the begin-
ning letter of each day's
name to the beginning
letters of children's names.

Monday / Maria
Tuesday / Tom

Daily Message

Interactive Writing Ask children
to write words in the message that
are on the Word Wall. Individuals
can write their names, too.

Today we will go to
the gym. We will see
a new book. Kevin
and Alan both
brought books they like.

From a pile of Letter Cards for *a, b, d, f, g, h, i, l, m, p, s,* and *t,* choose
children to hold up one letter at a time. The class finds and reads the Word
Wall words that begin with that letter. Briefly review that the words are in
ABC order.

Routines

 ## Daily Phonemic Awareness
Blending Phonemes

- Read "Hey, Diddle, Diddle" on page 32 of *Higglety Pigglety.*

- Play Mr. FunnyWord. *I'll read the poem again. When I stop, listen carefully for Mr. FunnyWord to say a word. Remember, he says words in a funny way. You put the sounds together and tell Mr. FunnyWord how to say it.*

- Stop before the word *cat.* **Here comes Mr. FunnyWord:** /c/ /a/ /t/. *What word should he say? That's right,* cat.

- Continue, having children blend *dog* and *ran.* If children need more practice, add these words for Mr. FunnyWord to learn: *bat, bit, jig, top, got, pig, at, if, lap.*

Higglety Pigglety: A Book of Rhymes, **page 32**

Getting Ready to Learn

To help plan their day, tell children that they will

- reread the Social Studies Link, *Ice Cream: From Cows to Kids!* and the Science Link, *Who Lives on the Farm?*

- learn to make and read new words in the Phonics Center.

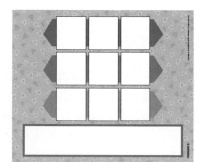

- read a book called "A Pot for Dan Cat."

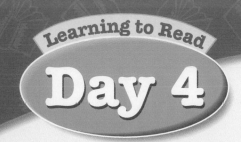

Big Book

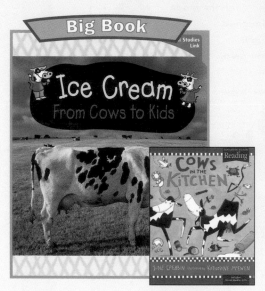

pages 27–33

Sharing the Big Books
Social Studies Link

▶ ## Building Background

Reading for Understanding Display _Ice Cream: From Cows to Kids!_ reminding children that they've heard this article before. Choose a child to tell what he or she learned about how ice cream is made.

page 28

Strategy: Monitor/Clarify

Student Modeling. _What could you do if you weren't sure what the farmer was doing on this page?_

pages 28–31

 ### Comprehension Focus: Drawing Conclusions

Student Modeling _Why do the farmer and other workers use machines? How do machines help?_ (Machines help make lots of ice cream at one time; they make it very fast.)

page 31
Concepts of Print: Directionality and Return Sweep

■ Read aloud and track the print. _Watch what happens when I get to the end of this line. Follow with your eyes. I'll read the next line and keep reading until I get to the end of the sentence. Who will try it while I read?_

▶ ## Responding

Summarizing Have children tell what they learned about making ice cream. List and number the steps on sentence strips and help children arrange them in order. Small illustrations will help them understand the order of the steps.

Science Link

▶ Building Background

Reading for Understanding Remind children that they also listened to *Who Lives on a Farm?* Choose a child to tell what he or she learned. Encourage others to add their ideas. Pause for discussion as you reread.

pages 29–35

Strategy: Evaluate

Student Modeling. *How did this article help us know more about the farm? Do you think the photographer and the writer gave us good information? What did you learn that you did not know before?*

page 31

Draw Conclusions: Make Inferences

■ *Name some jobs that a farmer does. Is being a farmer an easy job or a hard job? What do you think? Why?*

▶ Responding

Personal Response Talk about a farmer's job. Help children understand that it is hard work done by a skilled worker. Ask children what they've eaten today that came from a farm and represents the work of a farmer.

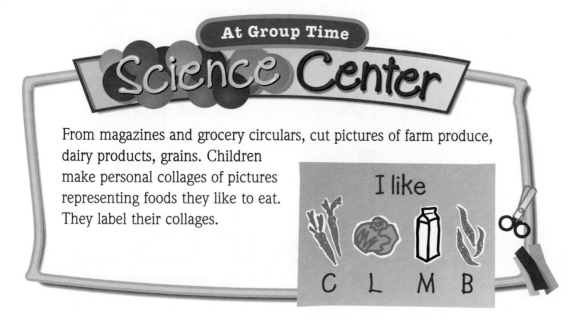

At Group Time

Science Center

From magazines and grocery circulars, cut pictures of farm produce, dairy products, grains. Children make personal collages of pictures representing foods they like to eat. They label their collages.

I like

C L M B

Big Book

Who Lives on the Farm?

MOUSE'S BIRTHDAY

Jane Yolen · Bruce Degen

pages 29–35

DAY 4

MEETING INDIVIDUAL NEEDS
Challenge

Search the library for picture books demonstrating how something is made. Look for topics of specific interest to your class. Encourage partners to view the books together and to tell each other and the group as a whole what they've learned.

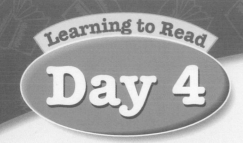

Day 4

OBJECTIVES

Children

- identify initial *f*, *h*, and *s* for words that begin with /f/, /h/, and /s/
- blend additional initial consonants with *-ox* and *-ot*

MATERIALS

- ***From Apples to Zebras: A Book of ABC's,*** pages 7, 9, 20
- **Alphafriend Cards** *Ozzie Octopus, Tiggy Tiger, Mr. X-Ray*
- **Letter Cards** *b, c, d, f, h, i, l, n, o, p, t, x*
- **Word Cards** assorted
- **Picture Card** *box*
- **Phonics Center:** Theme 8, Week 3, Day 4

Teacher's Note

During writing, if children ask how to spell words from the *-ox* or *-ot* family, refer them to the list of word family words in the Writing Center.

Home Connection

Remind parents to be on the lookout as they shop for items or names beginning with *f*, *h*, and *s*. Together, the family can make a game of their treasure hunt.

Phonics

✅ Blending -ox and -ot Words

▶ Connect Sounds to Letters

Review Consonants *f*, *h*, and *s* Have children locate the *F, f, H, h,* and *S, s* pages of *From Apples to Zebras.* To help them understand alphabetical order, have children tell how they know where to look for the pages. On each page, children point to the words and tell what they describe. Read the words as they point. Ask children what they notice about each word. (It begins with the target letter.)

From Apples to Zebras: A Book of ABC's

▶ Reviewing -ox and -ot

Hold up Letter Cards *o* and *x* **Listen: ox. Who will build the word with the Letter Cards? Now who will build pot? Say it slowly and use the letters you hear.**

Blending *-ox* and *-ot* Words With everyone writing the words, give these directions. *It's your turn now. Write not. Change pot to hot. (not, dot) Write a silly word. Write dox. Who ever heard of a dox? Let's change it to fox. Say the word slowly when you do it. Here are some more words to write:* lot, pox, got, box, cot, fox.

▶ Apply

Display the Picture Card *pot*, and have children help you build the word *pot* with Letter Cards. Then choose several children to *The pot is hot*. The group can help if needed. Build more words and sentences cooperatively, such as: *fox, The fox is not hot*. Children read the sentences aloud, smoothly and with expression.

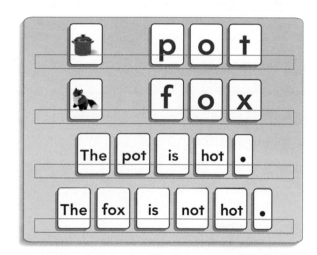

Practice Book page 251 Children will complete this page at small group time.

Phonics Library In groups today, children will also read *-ox* and *ot* in the **Phonics Library** story "The Big, Big Box." See suggestions, page T139.

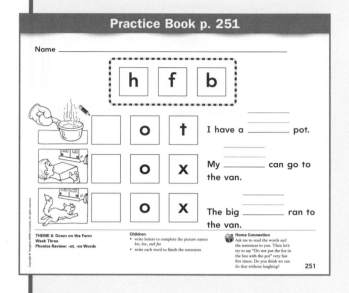

Phonics Center

Use the Phonics Center materials for **Theme 8, Week 3, Day 4**.

DAY 4

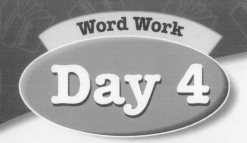

OBJECTIVES

Children

• build and read *-ig, -it, -ox* and *-ot* words

MATERIALS

• **Letter Cards** *b, c, d, f, g, h, i, l, n, o, p, r, s, t, x*

Building Words

▶ Word Families: *-ox, -ig, -it, -ot*

Distribute the Letter Cards to a group of children, one card per child.

■ *Who has the letters we need to write* ox? *Stand in front of the group.*

■ *Now, who will help them make* box? *Say the word slowly and to yourself. Who has the right letter?*

■ *Now change* box *to* pox.

■ *Here's a tricky one. Change* pox *to* pot. *Think about the sounds.*

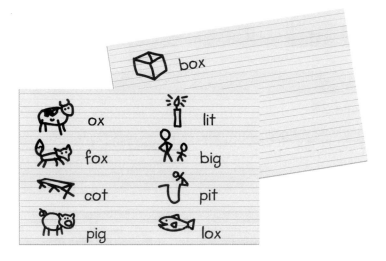

■ Continue, with children standing to make *not, hot, fox, lox, lot, rot.*

Small groups can enjoy working together to make a bank of words with word families they know: *-ox, -ot, -it,* and *-ig* words.

Children use Letter Cards to build *-ox, -ot, -ig,* and *-it* words. They can keep a list of their words to read to a partner.

pig	lit	cot	ox
big	pit	dot	fox
dig	bit	hot	box
fig	hit	pot	lox

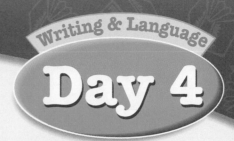
Interactive Writing

▶ Writing a Class Newsletter

Speaking and Writing Reread the Class Newsletter together. Tell children they'll write another article today. Together decide upon the subject. It can be a Center activity children enjoyed, a project, or an adventure children want to relate. Here are some suggestions for interactive writing.

- *What will we call our article? Remember that the title or headline should tell what the article is about.*

- *"Mr. Bunny's Birthday." That's a good title. Who will help me write the first letter in Bunny. Should it have a capital letter? Why?*

- *Benjamin can write his name for us. It starts with the same sound as Bunny, doesn't it?*

- *Who will help me write the word* like? *Remember to check the Word Wall to spell the word just right.*

- *If I didn't know how to spell* got, *what word on the Word Wall could help me?* (pot)

Read the completed article together.

Mr. Bunny's Birthday

We had a birthday party for Mr. Bunny.

He is 2 years old. Benjamin got him a new

box. Mr. Bunny likes lettuce and pellets.

We like to give him treats. We like Mr. Bunny.

HAPPY BIRTHDAY, MR. BUNNY!

OBJECTIVES

Children

- contribute ideas and share the writing of a newsletter article

DAY 4

Day 5

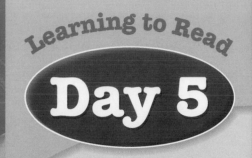

Day at a Glance

Learning to Read

Revisiting the Literature:

A Lion on the Path, Cows in the Kitchen, Mouse's Birthday, Ice Cream: From Cows to Kids!, Who Lives on the Farm?, and "A Pot for Dan Cat."

☑ **Phonics Review: Initial Consonants; *-ot* and *-ox* words;** *page T154*

Word Work

Building Words, *page T156*

Writing & Language

Independent Writing, *page T157*

  Half-Day Kindergarten

☑ Indicates lessons for tested skills. Choose additional activities as time allows.

Opening

Calendar

Sunday	Monday	Tuesday	Wednesday	Thursday	Friday	Saturday
			1	2	3	4
5	6	7	8	9	10	11
12	13	14	15	16	17	18
19	20	21	22	23	24	25
26	27	28	29	30	31	

Review the name of the month and the days of the week with children, along with any notations you've made on the calendar. Ask children to say something they've particularly enjoyed doing this month or in this theme about farm animals.

Daily Message

Modeled Writing Ask children to find and read words in the *-ot* word family in the message.

> We read a <u>lot</u> about farms and farm animals.
>
> Catrine <u>got</u> a new dog at her house.

Read the Word Wall together. Then play a guessing game: Read the wall again, after saying *I'm thinking of a word on the wall; the word is* said. *I am going to point to some words on the wall. Clap when you see me point to the word* said. Continue the game, using a few more words from the Word Wall.

Routines

✓ Daily Phonemic Awareness
Blending Phonemes

- Read "Humpty Dumpty" from page 19 of *Higglety, Pigglety*.

- Play a game with the poem. *Let's think about Humpty Dumpty. I'll give you some clues. You guess the answer by blending the sounds together.*

- *If Humpty had worn a hard / h / / a / / t /, he might be all right.* (hat)

- *The king had a lot of horses and a lot of / m / / e / / n /.* (men)

- *Humpty fell on this part of his head: / t / / o / / p /.* (top)

Humpty Dumpty

Humpty Dumpty sat on a wall.
Humpty Dumpty had a great fall.
All the King's horses and
all the King's men
Couldn't put Humpty
together again.

a Mother Goose Rhyme

Higglety Pigglety: A Book of Rhymes, page 19

Getting Ready to Learn

To help plan their day, tell children that they will

- revisit the books they've read.

- take home a story they can read on their own.

- write in their journals.

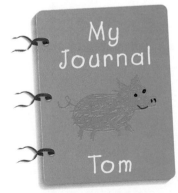

A Pot For Dan Cat
by Ann Spivey
illustrated by Gavin Bishop

Revisiting the Literature

▶ **Literature Discussion**

Today children will compare the books and articles they heard in this theme: *Mouse's Birthday, Who Lives on the Farm?, Cows in the Kitchen, Ice Cream: From Cows to Kids!, The Story of Half-Chicken,* and "Dot Got a Big Pot." First, browse through the literature together to help children recall what they've learned.

- Choose children to tell about the farm animals in the books.

- Have volunteers decide the stories that are make-believe and those that could really happen. Have children explain their reasoning.

- Browse through the illustrations in the Links. Ask individual children to retell the important information, using photographs to help them remember.

- Together, read "Dot Got a Big Pot." Call on individual children to point to and read -ot and -ox words.

 Comprehension Focus: Making Inferences

Help children use what they know to make inferences from a variety of texts. For example: *Knowing what you do about chickens, can a half-chicken really hop around and save fire, wind, and water? Why not? Is there really any such thing as a half-chicken?*

www.eduplace.com
Log on to **Education Place** for more activities relating to Down on the Farm.

www.bookadventure.org
This Internet reading-incentive program provides thousands of titles for children to read.

To Fan Fox
On My Way Practice Reader

▶ Preparing to Read

Building Background Tell children that this story is about a character they have met before, and ask if they remember her name. (Fan Fox) Explain that this time a uniformed cat named Kit delivers some packages to Fan Fox.

▶ Guiding the Reading

Walk through the story, discussing the two scenes on each page. Use the ideas below to prepare children for reading on their own.

page 1: *When you read, look at the top picture first and read the line under it. What is Kit Cat delivering? Read the label. Now look at the bottom picture. What was in the package? The folding bed is a cot. Does Fan Fox like it? Why?*

page 2: *What did Fan get this time? This fruit is called a fig. Find that word. Does Fan like the fig?*

pages 3-6: *For each page have children tell what Kit Cat delivers, point to the word that names it, and tell what Fan Fox thinks.*

page 7: *What did Fan Fox do with everything? Point to the cart. It has wheels. Can you find the word cart?*

Prompting Strategies Listen and observe children as they "whisper read." Use prompts such as these to help them apply strategies:

- *Read that line again and say the sounds in the word that gave you trouble.*
- *That word is on the Word Wall. Do you remember it?*
- *You said _____. Does that have the right sounds? Does it make sense?*

▶ Responding

Have partners take turns reading the story aloud, alternating scenes on each page. Encourage them to use their voices to show how the characters feel.

DAY 5

Home Connection

Remind children to share the **take-home** version of "To Fan Fox" with their families.

Revisiting the Literature/
Building Fluency   **T153**

Day 5

Phonics

✓ Consonants, Word Families

▶ Review

Tell children that they'll take turns being word builders and word readers. Have word builders stand with you at the chalkboard.

- *We'll write the word* ox. *Count the sounds you hear. Then write.*

- Word readers read the word in their places.

- Ask word builders what letter they'll need to make *box*. Children write the word and the word readers read what they've written.

- A new group changes places with the first one. They erase the *b*, write *f*, and ask the word readers to say the new word.

- Continue until everyone has built a word by replacing one letter. Examples: *box, fig, pot, pig, dot, dig, lox, dig, fox.*

High-Frequency Word Review

☑️ *I, see, my, like, a, to, and, go, is, here, for, have, said, the*

▶ Review

Give small groups sets of Word Cards, Picture Cards, and Punctuation Cards to make sentences. Children decide on the sentence, organize themselves, and stand in place for others to read their sentence.

▶ Apply

Practice Book page 252 Children can complete this page independently and read it to you during small group time.

Phonics Library Have children take turns reading aloud to the class. Each child might read one page of "To Fan Fox" or a favorite **Phonics Library** selection from the previous theme. Remind readers to share the pictures!

Discussion questions:

- *Choose a sentence and point to each word as you read.*

- *Find a word in "To Fan Fox" that begins with the same sound as Fifi Fish's name. What is the letter? What is the sound?*

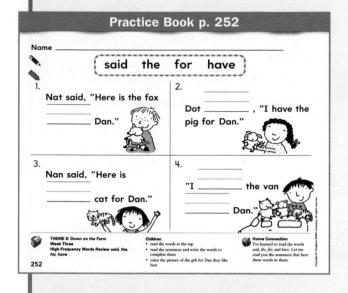

Practice Book p. 252

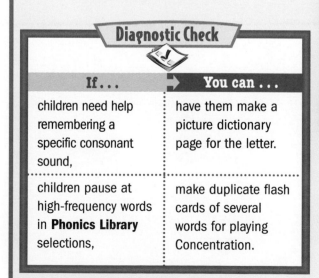

Portfolio Opportunity

Make a copy of the **take-home version** of "A Pot for Dan Cat" to tuck into each child's portfolio. Date the book to show when he or she learned to read it fluently.

Diagnostic Check

If . . .	You can . . .
children need help remembering a specific consonant sound,	have them make a picture dictionary page for the letter.
children pause at high-frequency words in **Phonics Library** selections,	make duplicate flash cards of several words for playing Concentration.

DAY 5

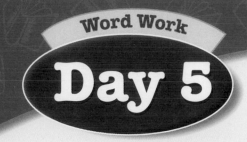

Day 5

Children

- build and read *-ig, -ot,* and *-ox* words

Building Words

▶ Word Families: *-ig, -ot, -ox*

Comment on how many words children can read and write now that they have learned words from the *-ig, -ot,* and *-ox* families. Give these clues and have children write the words:

- ■ *Write the name of an animal that ends with -ox.* (*fox*)

- ■ *This is a small, light bed.* (*cot*)

- ■ *This word means not little, but ... .* (*big*)

- ■ *This is a cardboard carton.* (*box*)

- ■ *This means not stand, but ... .* (*sit*)

Have children check their answers it with partners. Children can then cut the words apart and sort them into word families. Children can transfer the words into a personal word bank and illustrate them.

Independent Writing

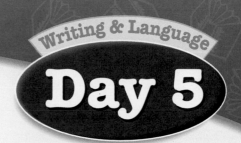
▶ Journals

Journals are multi-purpose books. They can be used to record information, keep track of observations in the Science Center, keep a personal word bank; for drawings, notes, creative writing; to practice handwriting, or just for fun. Set aside some time each day for children to write independently, making journal time special. Encourage children to write about something of their own choosing. If they are "stuck" for a topic, suggest that they peruse the classroom for the words, lists, charts, drawings, and books to spark an idea. They could draw something and then write about it. For more help, post this list of ideas in the Writing Center. Change the list frequently.

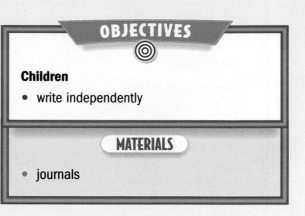

OBJECTIVES

Children
- write independently

MATERIALS
- journals

DAY 5

Theme Assessment Wrap-Up

Emerging Literacy Survey

Areas Assessed:

1. Concepts of Print
- Letter name knowledge
- Sound-letter association

2. Phonemic Awareness
- Rhyme
- Beginning sounds
- Blending onsets and rimes
- Segmenting onsets and rimes
- Blending phonemes
- Segmenting phonemes

3. Beginning Reading and Writing
- Word recognition
- Word writing
- Sentence dictation
- Oral reading

▶ Monitoring Literacy Development

If you have administered the **Emerging Literacy Survey** as a baseline assessment of the skills children brought with them to Kindergarten, this might be a good time to re-administer all or part of it to chart progress, to identify areas of strength and need, and to test the need for early intervention.

Use the **Observation Checklist** throughout the theme to write notes indicating whether each child has a beginning, developing, or proficient understanding of reading, writing, and language concepts. (See facing page.)

▶ Assessing Student Progress

Formal Assessment The **Integrated Theme Test** and the **Theme Skills Test** are formal assessments used to evaluate children's performance on theme objectives.

- The **Integrated Theme Test** assesses children's progress as readers and writers in a format that reflects instruction. Simple decodable texts test reading skills in context.

- The **Theme Skills Test** assesses children's mastery of specific reading and language arts skills taught in the theme.

Observation Checklist

Name _____   Date _____

	Beginning	Developing	Proficient
Listening Comprehension • Participates in shared and choral reading			
• Listens to story attentively			
Phonemic Awareness • Can blend phonemes			
• Can identify beginning sounds			
Phonics • Can recognize final *x*			
• Can build words with word family *-ox*			
Concepts of Print • Recognizes use of all capital letters			
• Can demonstrate reading direction; and return sweep			
Reading • Can read simple decodable texts			
• can read the high-frequency words *said, the*			
Comprehension • Distinguishes fantasy from realism in text			
• Notes important details			
• Can draw conclusions			
Writing and Language • Can draw and label images			
• Can write simple phrases or sentences			
• Can participate in shared and interactive writing			

For each child, write notes or checkmarks in the appropriate columns.

Theme Resources

Resources for *Down on the Farm*

Contents

Hush! Little Baby

Use this music for Mr. X-ray's song.

Down in the Valley

Folk Song

Use this music for Ozzie Octopus's song.

Old MacDonald

Word List

In Themes 1 through 3, the Phonics Library stories are wordless.

Theme 1

▶ **Phonics Skills:** none taught in this theme
▶ **High-Frequency Words:** none taught in this theme

Phonics Library, Week 1:
We Go to School
wordless story

Phonics Library, Week 2:
See What We Can Do
wordless story

Phonics Library, Week 3:
We Can Make It
wordless story

Theme 2

▶ **Phonics Skills:** Initial consonants s, m, r
▶ **High-Frequency Words:** I, see

Phonics Library, Week 1:
My Red Boat
wordless story

Phonics Library, Week 2:
Look at Me
wordless story

Phonics Library, Week 3:
The Parade
wordless story

Theme 3

▶ **Phonics Skills:** Initial consonants t, b, n
▶ **High-Frequency Words:** my, like

Phonics Library, Week 1:
The Birthday Party
wordless story

Phonics Library, Week 2:
Baby Bear's Family
wordless story

Phonics Library, Week 3:
Cat's Surprise
wordless story

Theme 4

▶ **Phonics Skills:** Initial consonants h, v, c; words with -at
▶ **High-Frequency Words:** a, to

Phonics Library, Week 1:
Nat at Bat
Words with -at: at, bat, hat, Nat, sat
High-Frequency Words: my, see

Phonics Library, Week 2:
A Vat
Words with -at: hat, mat, rat, vat
High-Frequency Word: a

Phonics Library, Week 3:
Cat Sat
Words with -at: bat, cat, hat, mat, sat
High-Frequency Words: my, see

Theme 5

▶ **Phonics Skills:** Initial consonants p, g, f; words with -an
▶ **High-Frequency Words:** and, go

Phonics Library, Week 1:
Nat, Pat, and Nan
Words with -an: Nan, ran
Words with -at: Nat, Pat, sat
High-Frequency Words: and, see

Phonics Library, Week 2:
Go, Cat!
Words with -an: Nan, ran, Van
Words with -at: Cat, Pat, sat
High-Frequency Word: go

Phonics Library, Week 3:
Pat and Nan
Words with -an: fan, Nan, ran
Words with -at: Pat, sat
High-Frequency Words: a, and, go

Theme 6

▶ **Phonics Skills:** Initial consonants l, k, qu; words with -it
▶ **High-Frequency Words:** is, here

Phonics Library, Week 1:
Can It Fit?
Words with -it: fit, it, sit
Words with -an: can, man, van
High-Frequency Words: a, go, I, is, my

Phonics Library, Week 2:
Kit
Words with -it: bit, fit, it, Kit, lit, sit
Words with -an: can, pan
Words with -at: hat
High-Frequency Words: a, here, I

Phonics Library, Week 3:
Fan
Words with -it: bit, quit
Words with -an: an, Fan
Words with -at: sat
High-Frequency Words: a, here, is

Theme 7

▶ **Phonics Skills:** Initial consonants d, z; words with -ig
▶ **High-Frequency Words:** for, have

Phonics Library, Week 1:
Big Rig
Words with -ig: Big, dig, Rig
Words with -it: pit
Words with -an: can, Dan
High-Frequency Words: a, for

Phonics Library, Week 2:
Tan Van
Words with -ig: Pig, Zig
Words with -it: it
Words with -an: can, Dan, ran, tan, van
Words with -at: Cat, sat
High-Frequency Words: a, have, I, is

Phonics Library, Week 3:
Zig Pig and Dan Cat
Words with -ig: dig, Pig, Zig
Words with -it: it
Words with -an: can, Dan
Words with -at: Cat, sat
High-Frequency Words: and, for, have, here, I, is

Theme 8

▶ **Phonics Skills:** Consonant x; words with -ot, -ox

▶ **High-Frequency Words:** said, the

Phonics Library, Week 1:
Dot Got a Big Pot

Words with -ot: Dot, got, hot, lot, pot
Words with -ig: big
Words with -it: it
Words with -an: Nan
Words with -at: Nat, sat
High-Frequency Words: a, and, I, is, like, said

Phonics Library, Week 2:
The Big, Big Box

Words with -ox: box, Fox
Words with -ot: not
Words with -ig: big
Words with -it: bit, fit, hit, it
Words with -an: can, Dan, Fan
Words with -at: Cat, hat, mat, sat
High-Frequency Words: a, is, my, said, the

Phonics Library, Week 3:
A Pot for Dan Cat

Words with -ot: pot
Words with -ox: Fox
Words with -ig: big
Words with -it: fit
Words with -an: can, Dan, Fan, ran
Words with -at: Cat, sat
High-Frequency Words: a, and, see, said

Theme 9

▶ **Phonics Skills:** Initial consonants w, y; words with -et, -en

▶ **High-Frequency Words:** play, she

Phonics Library, Week 1:
Get Set! Play!

Words with -et: get, set, wet, yet
Words with -ot: got, not
Words with -ox: Fox
Words with -ig: Pig
Words with -an: can
High-Frequency Words: a, play, said

Phonics Library, Week 2:
Ben

Words with -en: Ben, Hen, men, ten
Words with -et: get, net, pet, vet, yet
Words with -ot: got, not
Words with -ox: box, Fox
Words with -it: it
Words with -an: can
High-Frequency Words: a, I, my, play, said, she, the

Phonics Library, Week 3:
Pig Can Get Wet

Words with -et: get, wet
Words with -ot: got, not
Words with -ig: big, Pig, wig
Words with -it: sit
Words with -an: can
Words with -at: Cat, sat
High-Frequency Words: a, my, play, said, she

Theme 10

▶ **Phonics Skills:** Initial consonant j; words with -ug, -ut

▶ **High-Frequency Words:** are, he

Phonics Library, Week 1:
Ken and Jen

Words with -ug: dug
Words with -en: Ken, Jen
Words with -et: wet
Words with -ot: hot
Words with -ig: big, dig
Words with -it: it, pit
High-Frequency Words: a, and, are, is

Phonics Library, Week 2:
It Can Fit

Words with -ut: but, nut
Words with -ug: jug, lug, rug
Words with -ox: box
Words with -ot: not
Words with -ig: big
Words with -it: fit, it
Words with -an: can, tan, van
Words with -at: fat, hat
High-Frequency Words: a, he, see, she

Phonics Library, Week 3:
The Bug Hut

Words with -ut: but
Words with -ug: Bug, hug, lug
Words with -ox: box
Words with -ot: Dot, got, not
Words with -ig: Big, jig
Words with -an: can, Jan
Words with -at: fat, hat
High-Frequency Words: a, here, is, she, the

Cumulative Word List

By the end of Theme 10, children will have been taught the skills necessary to read the following words.

Words with -at
at, bat, cat, fat, hat, mat, Nat, Pat, rat, sat, vat

Words with -an
an, ban, can, Dan, fan, Jan, man, Nan, pan, ran, tan, van

Words with -it
bit, fit, hit, it, kit, lit, pit, quit, sit, wit

Words with -ig
big, dig, fig, jig, pig, rig, wig, zig

Words with -ot
cot, dot, got, hot, jot, lot, not, pot, rot, tot

Words with -ox
box, fox, ox

Words with -et
bet, get, jet, let, met, net, pet, set, vet, wet, yet

Words with -en
Ben, den, hen, Jen, Ken, men, pen, ten

Words with -ug
bug, dug, hug, jug, lug, mug, rug, tug

Words with -ut
but, cut, hut, jut, nut, rut

High-Frequency Words
a, and, are, for, go, have, he, here, I, is, like, my, play, said, see, she, the, to

Technology Resources

American Melody
P. O. Box 270
Guilford, CT 06473
800-220-5557

Audio Bookshelf
174 Prescott Hill Road
Northport, ME 04849
800-234-1713

Baker & Taylor
100 Business Court Drive
Pittsburgh, PA 15205
800-775-2600

BDD Audio
1540 Broadway
New York, NY 10036
800-223-6834

Big Kids Productions
1606 Dywer Avenue
Austin, TX 78704
800-477-7811
www.bigkidsvideo.com

Blackboard Entertainment
2647 International
Boulevard
Suite 853
Oakland, CA 94601
800-968-2261
www.blackboardkids.com

Books on Tape
P. O. Box 7900
Newport Beach, CA 92658
800-626-3333

Filmic Archives
The Cinema Center
Botsford, CT 06404
800-366-1920
www.filmicarchives.com

Great White Dog Picture Company
10 Toon Lane
Lee, NH 03824
800-397-7641
www.greatwhitedog.com

HarperAudio
10 E. 53rd Street
New York, NY 10022
800-242-7737

Houghton Mifflin Company
222 Berkeley Street
Boston, MA 02116
800-225-3362

Informed Democracy
P. O. Box 67
Santa Cruz, CA 95063
831-426-3921

JEF Films
143 Hickory Hill Circle
Osterville, MA 02655
508-428-7198

Kimbo Educational
P. O. Box 477
Long Branch, NJ 07740
900-631-2187

The Learning Company (dist. for Broderbund)
1 Athenaeum Street
Cambridge, MA 02142
800-716-8506
www.learningco.com

Library Video Co.
P. O. Box 580
Wynnewood, PA 19096
800-843-3620

Listening Library
One Park Avenue
Old Greenwich, CT 06870
800-243-45047

Live Oak Media
P. O. Box 652
Pine Plains, NY 12567
800-788-1121
liveoak@taconic.net

Media Basics
Lighthouse Square
P. O. Box 449
Guilford, CT 06437
800-542-2505
www.mediabasicsvideo.com

Microsoft Corp.
One Microsoft Way
Redmond, WA 98052
800-426-9400
www.microsoft.com

National Geographic Society
1145 17th Street N. W.
Washington, D. C. 20036
800-368-2728
www.nationalgeographic.com

New Kid Home Video
1364 Palisades Beach Road
Santa Monica, CA 90401
310-451-5164

Puffin Books
345 Hudson Street
New York, NY 10014
212-366-2000

Rainbow Educational Media
4540 Preslyn Drive
Raleigh, NC 27616
800-331-4047

Random House Home Video
201 E. 50th Street
New York, NY 10022
212-940-7620

Recorded Books
270 Skipjack Road
Prince Frederick, MD 20678
800-638-1304
www.recordedbooks.com

Sony Wonder
Dist. by Professional
Media Service
19122 S. Vermont Avenue
Gardena, CA 90248
800-223-7672

Spoken Arts
8 Lawn Avenue
P. O. Box 100
New Rochelle, NY 10802
800-326-4090

SRA Media
220 E. Danieldale Road
DeSoto, TX 75115
800-843-8855

Sunburst Communications
101 Castleton Street
P. O. Box 100
Pleasantville, NY 10570
800-321-7511
www.sunburst.com

SVE & Churchill Media
6677 North Northwest
Highway
Chicago, IL 60631
800-829-1900

Tom Snyder Productions
80 Coolidge Hill Road
Watertown, MA 02472
800-342-0236
www.tomsnyder.com

Troll Communications
100 Corporate Drive
Mahwah, NJ 07430
800-526-5289

Weston Woods
12 Oakwood Avenue
Norwalk, CT 06850-1318
800-243-5020
www.scholastic.com

Index

Boldface page references indicate formal strategy and skill instruction.

D

Decoding. *See* Phonics

    phonics/decoding strategy, **T35, T89, T139**

Details, noting important, related, and sufficient. *See* Comprehension skills.

Diaries and journals. *See* Journal.

Drama. *See* Creative dramatics.

Drawing conclusions. *See* Comprehension skills.

E

English Language Learners, activities especially helpful for, *T28, T32, T45, T94, T144*

    background, building, *T10, T40, T62, T94, T116, T144*

Expanding literacy. *See* Skills links.

F

Fantasy and realism. *See* Comprehension skills.

Fluency

    reading, *T49, T103*

G

Grammar and usage

    speech, parts of. *See* Speech, parts of.

Graphic information, interpreting

    calendars, *T8, T16, T26, T38, T46, T60, T71, T80, T92, T100, T114, T124, T134, T142, T150*

Guided Reading. *See* Coached Reading.

H

Handwriting, *T21, T75, T129*

High-frequency words

    a, **T14, T51, T68, T105, T122, T155**

    and, **T14, T51, T68, T105, T155**

    for, **T51, T105, T122, T155**

    go, **T51, T105, T155**

    have, **T51, T105, T155**

    here, **T14, T51, T105, T155**

    I, **T14, T51, T68, T105, T122, T155**

    is, **T14, T51, T68, T105, T155**

    like, **T51, T68, T105, T155**

    my, **T14, T51, T105, T122, T155**

    said, **T22, T23, T24, T51, T105, T122, T130, T131, T132, T155**

    see, **T14, T51, T105, T122, T155**

    the, **T76, T78, T122, T130, T131, T132, T155**

    to, **T51, T68, T78, T105, T155**

Home connection, *xiii, T35, T42, T49, T89, T103, T120, T139, T146, T153*

I

Independent and recreational reading

    self-selected, *xiv*

    suggestions for, *xiv*

Independent writing

    suggestions for, *T53, T107, T157*

Individual needs, meeting

    Challenge, *T31, T41, T87, T95, T127, T145*

    English Language Learners, *T10, T28, T32, T40, T43, T62, T96, T118, T144, T147*

    Extra Support, *T19, T34, T82, T85, T88, T123, T126, T128, T133, T137, T138*

Inferences, making, *T29, T152*

    drawing conclusions, *T116, T126, T127, T136, T137, T145*

Informational selection, structure of. *See* Comprehension, text organization.

Interactive writing, *xiv, T45, T46, T99, T100, T114, T142, T149*

Invented spelling. *See* Phonetic spelling.

J

Journal, *T53, T107, T157*

Judgments, making. *See* Comprehension skills.

K

Knowledge, activating prior. *See* Background, building.

L

Language concepts and skills

    exact words, *T69*

    language patterns, *T86*

Language mechanics. *See* Mechanics, language.

Leveled books

    Houghton Mifflin Classroom Bookshelf, *3, T49, T103, T153*

    Little Big Books, *3, T49, T103, T153*

    Little Readers for Guided Reading, *3, T49, T103, T153*

    On My Way Practice Reader, *3*

    Phonics Library, *2, 3, T43, T49, T51, T89, T97, T105, T139, T155*

Limited English proficient students. *See* English Language Learners.

Listening

    for rhymes, *T86*

    purpose

        to compare sounds, *T13*

        to discriminate sounds, *T13, T121*

    to an audiotape. *See* Audiotapes.

    to a read aloud. *See* Read Aloud selections.

    to creative dramatics. *See* Creative dramatics.

Literary devices

    sound words, *T84*

Literature

    discussion. *See* Responding to literature.

opening, *T8–T9, T16–T17, T26–T27, T38–T39, T46–T47, T60–T61, T70–T71, T80–T81, T92–T93, T100–T101, T114, T124–T125, T134–T135, T142–T143, T150–T151*

S

Science. *See* Cross-curricular links.

Self-correcting reading strategy. *See* Strategies, reading.

Sentence building, *T14, T22, T24, T51, T76, T78, T97, T105, T122, T130, T132, T155*

Sequence of events, noting. *See* Comprehension skills.

Shared writing, *T37, T91, T141*

Sight words. *See* High-frequency words.

Skills links
science, *2, T94–T95, T145*
social studies article, *2, T40–T41, T144*

Social Studies. *See* Cross-curricular links.

Speaking activities
describe people, places, things, number words, T116
dramatics. *See* Creative dramatics.
retelling. *See* Retelling.
summary. *See* Summarizing, oral summaries.

Speech, parts of
adjectives
comparative, *T16, T26, T38, T46*
nouns, *T15, T45, T69, T99, T123, T133*

Storytelling. *See* Retelling.

Strategies, reading
Evaluate, *T116, T126, T136, T137, T145*
Monitor/Clarify, *T10, T18, T29, T40, T144*
Phonics/Decoding, *T35, T89, T139*

Question, *T62, T72, T83, T85, T94*
Summarize, *T41*

Summarizing
oral summaries, *T41, T144*

T

Teacher-guided reading. *See* Coached Reading; Reading modes.

Teacher's Note, *xv, T6, T11, T21, T42, T53, T58, T63, T75, T86, T96, T107, T112, T117, T122, T129, T137, T146*

Teaching and management
managing program materials, *T112*
special needs of students, meeting. *See* Individual needs, meeting.

Technology resources, *xiii, T48, T102, T152, R8*

Text organization and structure. *See* Comprehension skills.

Theme
launching the, *xii–xiii*
projects, *xiii*
resources, *R1–R8*

Think Aloud. *See* Modeling, teacher.

V

Vocabulary, extending
days of the week, *T124, T142, T150*
months of the year, *T134, T150*
rhyming words, *T25*
weather words, *T16, T26, T38, T46, T60, T70, T80, T92, T100*
See also Language concepts and skills.

Vocabulary, selection
high-frequency words. *See* High-frequency words.

W

Word building, *T36, T42–T43, T44, T50, T52, T90, T96, T98, T104, T106, T140, T146, T147, T148, T154, T156*

Word wall, *T8, T16, T22, T26, T34, T38, T46, T60, T70, T76, T80, T88, T92, T100, T114, T124, T130, T134, T138, T142, T150*

Writer's craft
capitalization for emphasis, *T30, T85*

Writer's log. *See* Journal.

Writing activities and types
cooperative writing. *See* Shared writing.
diaries, logs, and notebooks, *T53, T107, T157*
independent. *See* Independent writing.
interactive. *See* Interactive writing.
letters and cards, *T91, T99*
note, *T99*
story, *T37*

Writing skills
formats. *See* Writing activities and types.
prewriting skills
story starters, *T37*